Don't
Look at the Camera

Don't
Look at the Camera

HARRY WATT

Paul Elek
LONDON

Published in Great Britain 1974 by
Elek Books Limited
54–58 Caledonian Road, London N1 9RN

ISBN 0 236 17717 6

Printed in Great Britain by
Ebenezer Baylis and Son Limited
The Trinity Press, Worcester, and London
Set in 11 pt. Baskerville, 1 pt. leaded

Harry Watt's Films

GPO FILM UNIT AND CROWN FILM UNIT PERIOD:

1934 *Six-Thirty Collection* (with Edgar Anstey)
      Radio Interference
1935 *BBC—Droitwich*
1936–37 Two items for *March of Time* (Second year Nos 3 and 4)
1936 *Night Mail* (with Basil Wright)
      The Saving of Bill Blewett
1938 *North Sea*
      Big Money
      Health in Industry (lost)
1939 *The First Days* (with Cavalcanti, Jennings and Jackson)
1940 *Squadron 992*
      Dover—Front Line
      London Can Take It (with Humphrey Jennings)
      Christmas Under Fire
1941 *War and Order*
      Target for Tonight
1942 *21 Miles* (Army Film Unit)

EALING PERIOD:

1942 *Nine Men*
1944 *Fiddlers Three*
1946 *The Overlanders*
1948 *Eureka Stockade*
1951 *Where No Vultures Fly*
1953 *West of Zanzibar*
1958 *People Like Maria* (Worldwide Films for World Health Organization)

1959 *The Siege of Pinchgut* (Associated British Distributors)
1962 *Dea Huide Hingst* (The Boy Who Loved Horses) Latevna Films

List of Illustrations

vii

I would like to acknowledge the considerable help and cooperation I have had on this book from Mike Weaver of the University of Exeter, Axel and Rossie Poignant, Frank Bryce, Jonah Jones, and the research departments of the British Film Institute and the Imperial War Museum.
I am also grateful for permission to reprint part of a film review from the *Manchester Guardian* (March 1935), two articles I wrote for the *Daily Express* (November 1941 and January 1942), and extracts from an article by Bernard Miles in *Documentary News Letter*; and to the Central Office of Information for allowing me to reproduce the poem 'Night Mail' by W. H. Auden. Lastly I would like to thank Therese Denny for her unfailing encouragement and enthusiasm to make me get on with it.

H.W.

I

Film memoirs, at least American ones with total recall about early childhood, seem fashionable. Unfortunately, the ones I come across always seem to start with Momma, surrounded by masses of food with names like gevultafish or sow's belly, bullying her son to study so that he won't end up as Poppa, who either drinks moonshine or sews on fly-buttons in a basement sweatshop. Our hero generally arrives in Hollywood, where he dreams of his Momma's cooking while screwing the starlets.

I will try and avoid this formula. Anyway, my mother wasn't much of a cook.

My father must have been one of the real boys-around-the-town of Glasgow. He was national hurdles champion, and played for Queen's Park, the crack amateur football team. He had dressed the part—huge checks, collars up to the ears, ulsters down to the ground, buttoned boots, and grey bowlers. He generally also sported a flower in his buttonhole the size of a small cabbage. Unfortunately for me, he continued to dress like this all his life. As a confident extrovert, he never realized he looked like a stage bookie, and revelled in the sensation his appearance made. As a horribly conventional self-conscious small boy, my principal memory is of walking with my father through the grim tenement streets of Scotland, with the chiacking coming from each entry 'Two to one, bar one, two to one the field'. Or kids of my own age following close behind us chanting 'Where did you get that hat?' My father loved it all and became as well-known a figure in Glasgow as the Celtic and Rangers players. Wherever you went you heard the whisper 'That's Harry Watt (rhyming in Scots with fat)—the MP.' He was a cartoonist's dream, and lots of sketches of him appeared in *Punch*. But it affected our relationship a lot.

To my shame, I progressively avoided going out with him, and this alienated us, and we never became intimate. This was terribly sad, as I realize now what a lovely man he was, and what a wonderful companion he would have been.

My mother was one of a clutch of beautiful Irish girls that came over from Dromore, County Down, presumably to find husbands. My father had just qualified in law when they married, and they must have had a thin time at first, as my father sat around for two years waiting for briefs, and became what they call in Scotland 'a stickit barrister'. They had one daughter, who was a very sickly child, so they decided to have no more. (Actually, my sister, twelve years older than me, turned into a remarkable woman, taking a first-class agricultural degree, introducing white turkeys into Scotland, and making enough money to set off round the world, working in Canada, Australia and South Africa before settling down.) Then my father turned to politics, the home-from-home of failed legal eagles. (Apart from politics, I think the film business is the other career where mediocrity flourishes.) He was eventually elected, as a Liberal, for the College Division of Glasgow, in 1905. Excited by the victory and unaccustomed champagne, my parents celebrated again in bed, and forgot to take the usual precautions. In the morning, when my mother reminded my father of this, he laughed and said 'Oh well, if it's a boy, we'll call him College.' It was a boy, and thank God, they called him Raymond Harry. (It is interesting that my mother, a reasonably sophisticated person, but tremendously inhibited about sex, only told me this story after I was married, aged twenty-five.)

Although he was intelligent and an excellent speaker, my father's career in Parliament was rather undistinguished. It was spoilt in a rather extraordinary way, that shows up the superficiality of the values in The House. When he started to speak, he made an immediate uproarious success as a funny man. He had them in the aisles, and a new star was born. A new comedian. 'Watt's going to speak, let's adjourn the committee and go in and have a good laugh.' But my father was sincere in his political beliefs, so he soon tired of being a comic, and took up the causes of his dreadfully poor constituency, and the Scottish nation. The members said 'Oh God, Watt was boring today, wasn't he?' and drifted away, and my father became a regular back-bencher, albeit always an active one. He was an ardent anti-Royalist, and annually proposed that their allowances should be cut, for which I have always admired him very much.

At the age of ten I was sent to Dollar Academy, one of several strange boarding schools scattered around Scotland. They are all founded and financed by the fortunes of awful old reprobates who have gone abroad—or to England—and exploited the locals. Dollar, in a tiny village in Clackmannanshire, was started by a privateer. Although large and impressively neoclassical, the village children could attend free. So I can remember kids with bare feet pattering into its marbled halls. It never seemed to occur to the authorities to provide them with boots!

As soon as I got to Dollar, I developed into a chronic asthmatic, so have few memories except illness. The one personality that remains in my mind is the matron of the house where I boarded, Ma Heyworth. She was a tiny dynamo of a widow, who had taken the job to get education for her two sons. Roger, her eldest, was head of the house in my last year. Madly ambitious for her children, particularly Roger, but without money or influence, she looked around for somewhere to place them and somehow hit on Lever Bros. She took herself off to Liverpool and demanded to see Lord Leverhulme. It is said she sat outside his office for days, and refused to be fobbed off by underlings. Eventually, when she saw the great man, she said 'I have a brilliant son, and I want you to give him a chance.' Lord Leverhulme is said to have replied 'Madam, if he has anything of your perseverance and personality, I'll gladly take him on.' Roger Heyworth became Lord Heyworth, and the head of the whole concern.

Strangely enough, many years later, I sat beside him on a flight from Melbourne to Sydney, and reminded him of when he had caned my bottom. And such are the ridiculous values of the present day, on our arrival it was I the pressmen and photographers wanted to see, because I was a film director.

Because of my constant asthma, I was taken away from Dollar at thirteen, brought back to the family home in Edinburgh, and sent to a rather snobby middle-class school, Edinburgh Academy. My family were living apart by this time. My father kept buying small farms, and living on them when he wasn't in London. I imagine he had also been caught out in various peccadilloes with women—he didn't drink and although he liked women, I don't believe he was a womanizer—but my mother was such a Puritan, that a rather gushing letter from a female admirer could bring about a row. He had a sudden violent temper—which I inherited, as any of my film units can vouch for—and this led to a very happy period of my childhood.

We all went to a new farm my father had bought in Dumfriesshire and my maternal grandmother visited us. She and my father clashed for some reason, and he used some choice four-letter words. My mother muttered one of the famous clichés 'How dare you speak to my mother like that' and walked out, dragging me after her. But, being a considerable individual, she didn't just go home, but went straight across the lovely Moniaive valley, and rented another farm directly opposite my father's. This she proceeded to farm successfully for two years, while I ran wild on the hills (I did have tutors from time to time). I had dogs and ponies, and my friends were the poachers and farm workers, and I was as happy as I have ever been. My father rode over about twice a week to try and persuade my mother to chuck it, but she resolutely refused, and I imagine would never have joined up with him again, if her farm had not come on the market, and my father bought it over her head to get her back.

I somehow didn't enjoy the Edinburgh Academy much. I suppose my loyalties had been developed in a boarding school, and a day school was a come-down. However, without too much effort, I was consistently top of my class. No-one at home seemed very interested or impressed.

Only two episodes at the Academy remain at all vividly in my memory. The first was when I became the first active and vociferous Socialist in the school. I have no recollection of being suddenly converted to Socialism, but put myself up as the Socialist candidate in a mock election at the debating society on an anti-Royalist, Republican ticket! This, in a school for the sons of the solid burghers of Auld Reekie, was sensational stuff. And when, in the debate, I said that if the Royal Family were used by any opponents of my revolution as figureheads for a counter-revolution, they would have to be shot, I was up before

4

the head next day. I thought I was for the high-jump, but as I only got one vote—my own—in the final count, I imagine they felt my subversive potential was minimal.

The other episode was much more important, and affected my whole life for many years, in fact up to the moment when an extraordinary little Scots visionary called John Grierson said 'You'd better start on Monday.' He stopped me being an unambitious drifter, which I suddenly became at the age of sixteen, through the most well-meant and innocuous circumstances. In all the mush of school-life, I can remember the details completely.

As I have said, I was always top of my class. This was on the average of all subjects, although I was never beaten at English. It came about, I think, because I liked learning, read everything I could lay my hands on, and found the background and reason for learning stimulating. It was, I now sometimes think, a sort of latent instinct for journalism, which helped me so much later on. At the same time, I wasn't a 'swot'—I played rugger for the school, captained the Second XI, won the mile, all that sort of thing—and the swots of the classes, whom we rugger types bullied unmercifully, couldn't quite understand it. Anyway— and I must use all the names, because I remember them so clearly—we had an eccentric English master called 'Twank'. (His great moment for us was when he brought back a copy of the Bayeux Tapestry from one of his holidays and forgot to cut out the dirty bits.) He set us an extra prep of learning poetry —and, as we had three regular preps a night, the class agreed not to do Twank's extra stint. When we had to write it out, we cribbed it from the book. And one of the swots 'cliped', which is a Scots word for report or betray. I didn't give a damn—a beating maybe. But then I was summoned to my form-master, Billy Peel, a decent, upright and obviously stupid man. I was told that, as I had cheated, no matter where I came, I would not be placed first. I just shrugged to myself, and carried on as before. After the end of term exams, for which I had worked hard, as always, I was again summoned to Billy Peel's room. He started off 'I have got to say I admire you, Watt.' I preened. 'Despite what I told you a month ago, you have worked well, and came out easily first in the class. However, you cheated in your English poetry class and I have had to put you fourth in the rankings. But I want to say again how pleased I am with the way in which you have behaved.' I thanked him and left. Suddenly, halfway across the quadrangle, I stopped dead. I had a sudden revelation. 'I don't *need* to do all this bloody work. It doesn't matter. They've taken away my rightful position on the word of a round-shouldered, pebble-glassed little shit. So I'll never work hard again.' I never did. I disestablishmented myself. I staggered through around the middle for two more years without opening a book, to vague tut-tuts and the belief, I suppose, that I must have cribbed my way to the top in previous years. Nobody seemed to notice at home, and my drop-out attitude to ambition lasted for six years. What surprises me about this episode, which stays so vividly in my memory to this day, is that I never spoke about it to anyone, until I met the girl I eventually married. (It has been suggested that the impact of this event is the grounds for my anti-academic feelings, which made me a maverick in the intellectual arguments of the thirties.)

It had always been accepted that I would go to University. Again, it was a most casual affair. At the conventional farewell hand-shake with the Head, he suggested I should become a barrister, as I seemed to argue about everything. But I felt he was just glad to see the back of me. My father vaguely mentioned Cambridge, but when I said I wanted to go to Edinburgh —because I had pals there—he agreed. Nobody, astonishingly, discussed what I should read. What I wanted to do was to travel and see the world, so, because some pal in a pub said businessmen went everywhere, I registered for the Bachelor of Commerce course! As it turned out largely to be a course training young executives to administer large factories, and as I disliked big business both in fact and in principle, it was about as ridiculous a decision as I have ever made.

There then followed the most undistinguished University career it is possible to imagine. Not that I wasn't constantly active. I became the comedian in the annual revue, I was involved with the student magazine, I captained the rugby second XV, and got a half-blue—I also played for a midweek XV unofficially known as The Smokeroom Dregs. It sometimes contained international players, but as we were usually half-cut by the time we got on the field, our results were somewhat

6

unpredictable. I debated, and became a member of the University Labour Party, but not very seriously.

My main moments in it were during the Rectoral election. In those days the candidates were chosen purely to represent the three main political parties, so we met to choose a Socialist candidate and decided to invite Paul Robeson, the famous American negro singer and actor, who was in England. This was a remarkably advanced choice for that time. The usual candidates were successful politicians or local landed gentry and Robeson was a foreigner, black, and an alleged Communist. To us he was a spokesman and fighter for freedom.

I was sent South with another chap to ask Robeson if he would agree to stand as Lord Rector. It was my first foray into England, and we eventually landed up at Beaconsfield, where Robeson was making a film. Very shy and self-conscious, we were taken to a dressing-room which Robeson seemed to fill. He was an immense man, with tremendous natural authority, yet kind and warm. We explained our mission, and Robeson made us sit down while he pondered it. He then started to question us. 'Were there many coloured students at Edinburgh?' 'Yes', we said, 'it had the highest proportion of people from all parts of the Empire of any University.' 'Were there colour problems or prejudices?' he then wanted to know. 'There were none to speak of—oh, a few landladies, perhaps, but amongst the students there was no colour bar, complete integration.' Robeson got up, looked at us steadily for a moment and then said 'Please tell your Committee I am highly honoured by their invitation, but I cannot accept it.' He then went on to explain to us naïve kids what could happen in a liberal place like the Edinburgh we had described if a black man, and a Left-wing one at that, were chosen to compete for such a high position. All the freedom from prejudice that we had taken for granted might be lost for ever, and latent evils that existed everywhere could come to the surface and poison our easy-going world. He told us of his experiences in America until he was called onto the set, leaving the dressing-room tremendously empty and a couple of chastened youngsters who had, for the first time, met a great man.

I still think Robeson was right, although I'm sure present-day Black Power thinking will say that he ratted out of a tremendous chance to voice and represent black opinion. But at the Edinburgh University of that time, with many hundreds of overseas students of every shade—including a considerable number of black Americans—there was, in my memory, no colour bar or prejudice amongst the students. It was the most integrated atmosphere I have ever encountered. If a black man had stood for Lord Rector, the reactionaries would happily have bashed every black in sight, as they did the Socialists, and Edinburgh, the University of the Empire, would have been destroyed. It might also have affected history, for many of the leaders of the new independent African states were educated at Edinburgh.

During the fortnight before the voting for the Lord Rector, all other activities more or less stopped, and prolonged and sometimes vicious fights took place between the different factions.

The rugger-buggers were ninety per cent Tory, the huge Highland shinty players—they mostly were studying for the Ministry, if they failed they became policemen—were Liberal, and the Socialists just took it. So I formed a Labour Physical Force Gang, of which I was very proud. Its formation was announced at a regular meeting of the Party, and the Chairwoman, a certain Jenny Lee, arose in all her majesty and tore about the biggest strip off me that I'd ever had. Apparently, the policy of the Party at that time was pacifism. I took my lecture, went out into the night with my followers, and knocked hell out of some Tories.

I also disappointed my Labour friends by joining the University Officers Training Corps, purely because it was a horse-drawn light artillery detachment, and I wanted to get some riding. My career there ended typically. We went on a long weekend camp to Fife, and I, with two cronies, Bollocks Turnbull and a White Russian, Count de Soldenhoff, known, of course, as Bolshie, started a roulette school and won the enormous sum of £15. We then proceeded to try and paint the wretched local village red, and I ended up in the clink. I was said to have been picked up throwing split peas at the band in the school hall. I have often wondered where the hell I got the split peas.

I was dismissed from the Corps for 'behaviour unbecoming to

8

a gentleman', and, to my surprise, was welcomed on my return in disgrace by a deputation from the Labour Party, who congratulated me on escaping from the clutches of the military. I quietened down a bit when I took up boxing, and got to the finals of the middle-weights. Many years later this led to an odd moment of which I was very proud. I was location hunting alone in Uganda for my second African feature, *West of Zanzibar*, and stopped at a tiny pub right out in the bush. There was only one other white man in the bar, so naturally we got chatting. I recognized from his accent that he was Scots. When we exchanged names, he got quite excited and said 'I know you, I know you.' (I thought 'Here it comes'—'I saw *The Overlanders* and wasn't yon lassie—what was her name?—Daphne Campbell, that's it—wasn't she lovely?' So often, fans seemed only to remember the star's bust measurements.) But then I got a shock. He went on 'You were in the final of the middle-weights at Edinburgh in 1926!' This was about thirty years on, and I was enormously proud. To hell with the film business, he didn't even know I was in it! We went through the bout blow by blow and got gloriously drunk. It's a funny thing, but, although my mind knows what a horrible young man I was, my silly male ego still makes me rather proud of my misspent youth and my stupid exploits. It's all this boys-will-be-boys and sow-ing-wild-oats stuff, and is indefensible. Incidentally, of my three particular cronies, equally amoral, one was killed on a motor-bike, one committed suicide, and one became an admiral!

Then my father had a heart attack, and came home a very sick man. He was still in his early sixties. I was recalled from the University and we moved to a house on the Clyde. The sorry mess my academic life was in soon came out, and it was decided I would stay at home that summer and help my mother. It was the longest time we three had been together since I was nine. My father didn't attack me or criticize me. Although I admired him and liked him very much we had lost all intimacy, and were self-conscious in each other's presence. I imagine he just felt I was a wash-out, and not worth bothering about.

As I saw him fading away, I felt a great longing for the friendship we had never had. But it was too late, and I never raised the question of my personal problems. Yet I believe I would have done anything he suggested to justify myself in his eyes. What does surprise me, looking back, was that he never seemed to think of introducing me to his influential friends. I knew he knew top industrialists, bankers, Lord Provosts, and, of course, numbers of MPs. So it is strange that, with a family that had been in the centre of public life for twenty years, I never got one string pulled on my behalf. Maybe they just thought I would let them down.

I got restless again after a while and answered an advert in the *Glasgow Herald* for a representative. It was a dreadfully sleazy soft-goods firm in a back street slum, presided over by a very old vulture. He took me on at a tiny salary and commission, and I set off in my clapped-out car for the North-East. Although I sold very little, I enjoyed myself. I saw all the lovely fishing villages up the Aberdeenshire coast, and I entered into the ceremonial life of the commercial traveller—all, I imagine, now gone. We stayed in the same small hotels, and had our 'high tea' at one long table, with the oldest member taking the chair, and the others sitting in order of seniority down to me. The talk was serious, of percentages and expenses, and sometimes a small collection was made for the Widows and Orphans. Then we drifted off to write up our order books. There were no uproarious dirty jokes or pinching of maid's bottoms that I ever saw. I hadn't been so circumspect for years.

After my second trip north, I tried to get back from Inverness to Argyllshire in a day, ran into a snowstorm, and smashed my car up. I was promptly fired. That old Glasgow bastard had only taken me on because I had a car of my own, still a rarity for a young fellow in those days. (One of my father's great mistakes was letting me have his old car. There is a lot of talk of the laxity of young women's morals at the present day, but having a car at a Scottish university in the early twenties was as surefire a bait as a penthouse in the Kings Road today.)

I couldn't have carried on with my job anyway, because my father had brought himself to death's door looking for his burial place. In Scotland, ultimate death is accepted and discussed in great detail in the family. Later on, while my mother was hale and hearty, my sister and I knew exactly what was to be written on the tombstone, who was to be asked to the lunch afterwards, where they were to sit, 'the Minister at the head of the table', and even what was to be served. We were not to hand out whisky or 'cousin so-and-so, you know, might get drunk'. My father had become preoccupied with where he was to be buried, and finally settled on a beautiful little graveyard on the shores of the Holy Loch (now the base for American nuclear submarines). The cemetery stretched from the shore up into the hills, and my father couldn't make up his mind whether to lie by the church and the shore or to dominate the magnificent view. It always struck me as macabre, wanting a view from your coffin, but very Scots. Anyway, unbeknown to anyone, he hired a car and had himself driven to the graveyard, climbed the terribly steep hill, and collapsed with another heart attack, from which he died in a few weeks. The only final advice I can remember him giving me was 'Keep out of the hands of lawyers' and 'You'd better just live in the country', which showed, I suppose, what he really thought of me.

He left my mother comfortably off, and she retired to a bungalow, where she proceeded to lavish the pride and affection to his memory that she seemed to have been unable to show to him during his lifetime. Every lovely view was *his* view, every beautiful flower *his* favourite. It was very sad, but is, I'm afraid, all too common.

So now I was quite lost, and didn't know what the hell to do. I was thumbing through my mother's awful local rag 'Church Bazaar raises £7-14-8d for the orphans of Umpopoland', when I was suddenly stopped short by an item about a Newfoundland sailing schooner that had been picked up in distress off the very northern tip of Scotland and towed into Oban. It was news because there were women and children on board. I had always been keen about the sea, and had, in fact, made a trip in a trawler to Iceland when I was about sixteen, and I kept thinking about that schooner. When there was an item in the national press about the departure of the involuntary immigrants, some having found long-lost relatives, I had my revelation 'By God, the schooner will have to go back too' and set off for Oban. And there she was, sure enough, and loading.

She was a heavily built, but quite lovely, Danish fore-and-aft schooner of around 80 tons, which had been used on the salt-cod run from Newfoundland to Spain. Something had gone wrong in St John's, and she had been sold off cheap to the storekeeper of Newtown, a tiny village in the north, who had dodged up and down the coast with her in the summer carrying passengers and local goods. She had been caught in a famous westerly gale, and, losing most of her sails, drifted out into the Atlantic. The storekeeper-skipper decided to just run before the gale, and headed for what he thought would be England. His navigation was such that he very nearly missed Scotland. After his Atlantic crossing, he had had quite enough of the sea, and went home, but not before his trader's eye had spotted the bargains to be found in Scotland. So the schooner was being packed with, of all things, second-hand bicycles and sewing-machines!

I introduced myself to the new skipper, a retired sealer who had been sent over to sail the *Neptune* back. He agreed to sign me on as a deckhand at one dollar for the trip. This was to make me legal. I wanted to go, so didn't bargain, and started to hump bikes. The rest of the crew consisted of two young fishermen who had been on board when the schooner went adrift, and a sixteen-year-old half-wit son of the owner. One of the fishermen had been made mate, but couldn't navigate, so, if the skipper, who was about seventy, had collapsed on the trip, we'd have been back to square one.

We were due to sail in about a week's time, on 1 April, which brought plenty of cracks from the dockside watchers, who were fascinated by the number of old bicycles we kept stuffing into the hold. The two other young chaps were marvellous workers, and good seamen, but I found the Newfoundland dialect almost incomprehensible. It was based on a sort of archaic provincial English, with a strong Canadian overlay and lots of words cropped up that were now quite obsolete in our everyday speech. The half-wit was the usual good humoured butt, who tried his best to do odd jobs, but generally just got in the way.

The deckhands all shared the fo'c'sle, and the skipper had a tiny deck-cabin aft. A small auxiliary engine had been fitted in Oban, and this led to our adding to our crew at the last moment. It suddenly struck the skipper that none of us had the faintest idea how to run this engine, so he signed up a dreadful little dockside hanger-on. His Highland nickname was Gadgy, and he swore he was a qualified marine engineer. We all decided he was a no-good bum, and we were right.

When you're about twenty you don't make much preparation for a journey, even if it's sailing the Atlantic. I bought a cheap oilskin, some sea-boots, and a couple of sweaters. I forgot gloves, which made a lot of the trip hell. I'd begun to have grave suspicions about the grub. Hardly any stores seemed to be coming aboard, and the Newfoundlanders pointed to some greasy casks in the fo'c'sle when I questioned them, so I lashed out on tinned fruit and bully beef, and, on the day before we sailed, an enormous bottle of Bovril, which saved Gadgy's life.

By the time it came to batten down the hatches, the deck was still littered with bicycles. The skipper was ashore clearing the ship. We were all thoroughly sick of bikes by this time, so we piled the rest into the hold, and jumped on them. There was some awful grinding cracking noises, but the hatches were on when the old man came back.

Quite a crowd came to see us off, including an uncle of mine, who was convinced we would all be lost. Actually, the *Neptune* was a wonderfully seaworthy craft, but dreadfully slow. But it was early in the year to make the crossing against the prevailing winds.

We were well out off Ireland before we got anything like a blow, and the old skipper showed he was a careful sailor. As soon as the glass started to fall, he had sail taken off. He always wore a suit and a cloth cap, and, apart from the big old-fashioned leather sea-boots, could have been in charge of a dockside shop. He chewed tobacco constantly, and to my considerable surprise, spat on the deck. I had thought that, even in the scruffiest ships, this was a heinous crime. It also was a bloody nuisance, as I had to wash it off each day.

For the deck-hands, it was four hours on and four hours off, day and night. This actually meant the two Newfoundlanders and me, because Gadgy collapsed with dreadful seasickness as soon as we cleared land, and hardly appeared again. We had imagined that the half-wit could stand a watch as look-out forward, but when a fully lighted liner passed about half a mile away, and he failed to see it, we gave up. The old man seldom came on deck at night in fine weather, so generally the steersman was on his own. And that was where I realized what a mug I'd been about gloves.

The huge wooden wheel was just forward of the small deck-house on the poop, and fully exposed. One had to hold on hard with both hands to keep the schooner on course in any sort of a breeze, and the steersman constantly got showers of spray blown aft as she banged her blunt nose into the everlasting westerly swell. So it was cold, bitterly, horribly cold. And the further across we got the colder it became. I used to wear four pairs of socks on my hands when I was at the wheel, but when we went about, or shortened sail, I got soaked and that was it. As we generally slept in our clothes, it was a good thing we were young.

The grub soon turned out to be even worse than I had suspected. We quickly finished the ham that had hung in the fo'c'sle and the few dozen eggs stowed in the galley, and were forced back on the casks. This was the real original sailing-ship food on which, I suppose, the British won the Battle of Trafalgar. I can only vouchsafe that their stomachs must have been as strong as their hearts. It was ancient, half-bad greasy pork, and crumbling dry biscuits. No weevils, as far as I could see, but we were all suddenly overrun with bed-bugs. We used the old wartime method of running our fags up the seams of our clothes, and the bugs went pop. But when we began to explore where they had come from, we realized that our poor half-wit had not changed his clothes or aired his bed in the last six months. He was crawling, so we chucked his bedding and clothes over the side, and each subscribed a piece of something to take their place. He was even more of a scarecrow, but with a forced wash of paraffin and water, reasonably clean.

Working the ship was pretty easy, but what did frighten me was going out along the immense bowsprit to furl the foresails when we had our weekly gales. The bowsprit reared high over the bows, and when you looked along it from the eyes of the schooner, it seemed to go on for ever; so you gritted your teeth, and battled out along the loose foot-ropes. By this time the seas would have got up, so one moment you would be thirty or forty feet above the waves, and the next waist deep, as the old schooner buried her nose into it. The two Newfoundlanders used to sing and shout with the excitement of it. I just hung on and cursed.

All this time the wretched Gadgy lay in his bunk and retched. He could eat nothing, and was obviously becoming very weak. I resurrected my Bovril, and he managed to hold that down. In

14

fact, he became quite chipper, but resolutely refused to leave his bunk. This didn't worry us fo'c'sle hands much, but it must have irked the skipper, for he suddenly burst into our fuggy hideout, and told Gadgy that if he wasn't on deck in five minutes, he'd kick his face in. Poor Gadgy crawled on deck in his thin dungarees—he had no oilskins—and was promptly knocked over by a wave. We stuck him back below, and the old man ignored him from then on.

We had taken a very northerly route, and after about a month, we could sense that ice wasn't very far away. There was a scary sharpness in the wind, and a faint almost imperceptible lightening on the northern horizon. It was the Grand Banks area, and we soon ran into fog. We also got our first favourable breeze, and the old man promptly set all our sail. As we went tearing through the wet, cold impenetrable night, I asked the skipper what would happen if we hit ice. He spat reflectively and said 'The jibboom will be back on the poop.' It was the only joke he made to me, and it didn't make me laugh.

We made our landfall just north of St John's after six weeks out. To all our astonishments, the ice had not completely broken up, and lay, heaving and sullen, up to five miles off the coast. The mate, from the cross-trees, said there was a sort of a passageway close in, so at last Gadgy came into his own, and started the engine. It went fine, and we dodged along inshore for an hour or two until the ice got more and more solid. I suppose the old man was tired, and wanted to finish the trip, because he persevered with the motor, and suddenly there was a horrible bang aft, and the engine stopped. We had bashed the propeller on a small floe, and Gadgy was out of work again.

We spent a frustrating week trying to wind our way through the ice, making the odd mile, then getting stuck until a breeze opened out a channel again. One day, when we were surrounded by broken ice, we saw two figures coming out to us from the shore, jumping from floe to floe in a marvellously agile way. They turned out to be youngish Newfoundlanders, thin and tough-looking, but half starved. Their winter supplies had just about finished, and it was still too early to get to a store. We had nothing but the gruesome remains of the salt pork. The two were obviously so hungry and poor, that we mustered all our reserves of bully-beef and tinned fruit, and had our arrival

15

feast then and there. It was forty-five years ago, but I can still remember feeling moved and ashamed at seeing starving people trying to eat respectably, so as not to embarrass their hosts.

During the voyage, in the watches below, the Newfoundlanders had regaled me with the usual fo'c'sle descriptions of the girls at home, and what a reception we'd get. After six weeks at sea, I had high hopes of finding the village tart, or at least a compliant fisher girl. I got a shock when we at last sailed into Newtown Bay. About ten ramshackle clap-board houses perched right on the rocky shore. There was a tiny church, and a sort of large shed, which turned out to be the village store, run by the owner of the *Neptune*, and the dance hall schoolhouse, all rolled into one. There was a terrible sense of desolation. The snow was just melting. Behind and around the houses there were no gardens, no vegetable patches. Just quaking horrible tundra. It was somehow almost terrifying to realize that these people never grew anything, any time.

The roaring welcome I had expected resolved into a lot of hand-shaking, back slapping, and incomprehensible local jokes. And the girls were awful. Although the men were tall and handsome, the girls were white-faced anaemic little things, presumably because they could hardly ever leave their houses, and the diet they had to exist on. The only lovely things at Newtown were the two communally-owned schooners, in which the men sailed annually to the Grand Banks. These were the traditional Blue Nose type, which is one of the most beautiful craft in the world. It was strange that they could come out of such sordid ugliness.

The famous dance took place in the village hall. A jolly old one-eyed chap played the accordion. The girls crowded and giggled shyly at one end, in dreadful home-made cotton dresses. The men looked fine in their blue guernseys and thick strong tweed trousers. Physically they seemed a different race. Of course, Gadgy and I were objects of immense curiosity to the girls. We were the first people from another land they had ever seen. We eyed them over, and tried to decide which might have a spark of fun in them. Then the accordionist struck up, and we were surprised to see everyone lining up for a sort of barn dance, but dull and stylized, with none of the abandon that the

Southern American gets into them. These went on, and we were pushed through one or two. But we'd been given, on the sly, a shot or two of rum, and we wanted something a bit more intimate. So we asked for a waltz. To our utter astonishment, they neither knew the dance, nor even a waltz tune. And this was 1929. Both Gadgy and I were show-offs, and the rum was working well. So we started by singing, or rather humming, the Merry Widow Waltz over and over to the one-eyed accordionist, until he'd more or less got it. Then I took Gadgy in my arms— he was only about five-foot-two—and we solemnly waltzed round the hall, with me counting 'One, two, three; one, two, three', and Gadgy humming as loud as he could to keep the accordionist in tune. And nobody laughed. They were utterly fascinated, and you could see heads bobbing and hear whispered counting all through the crowd.

Then everybody had a go, and this was a riot, with more squeals and roars of delight than the village hall had ever heard. It was really daring. Look, we're waltzing! Newtown had entered the Twentieth Century.

I had to stay another week before I got a passage down the coast. I got more and more depressed with the miserable standard of life these friendly simple people seemed to have chosen for themselves. There appeared no reason for them to live in Newtown. It was even far from the fishing grounds, and for much of the year they were completely cut off. My most poignant memory was watching a young girl trapping tiny snow-birds, the harbingers of spring, and happily screwing their necks at the promise of the first fresh meat for six months.

The storekeeper gave me a gold five-dollar piece as a farewell gesture. Gadgy signed on with him as engineer. He wanted to save up to get to America. I often wondered if he ever got the engine going again.

I got a lift in a launch going down the coast to St John's, which turned out to be one of the arse-holes of the world. While hanging about there for a boat to Canada, I turned down an opportunity I've always regretted. I was offered a berth as a deck-hand on a rum-runner which meant sailing over to St Pierre Miquelon, the tiny French island in the Gulf of St Lawrence, and then shipping wines and brandy to Rum Row, off the US coast. The pay was good, the grub terrific and the risk small, I was told. Like a bloody young fool I turned it down because my sexual repressions, as they are now called, were so acute that I couldn't wait to get to Toronto, where a girl-friend of mine had recently emigrated. I'd love to have been able to drop into the conversation 'When I was a rum-runner . . .'

I finally got a small steamer to Montreal. I shared my cabin with a city slicker type, who was on his way to tear Canada, and then the States, apart. I, who was still a pretty naïve boy, listened fascinated to his easy plan of how to become a millionaire. When we got to Montreal it was still cold, and I wanted to get an overcoat, but cheap, as I was by now nearly broke. So my new-found friend took me to the Jewish second-hand clothing area, and when I fancied a coat, did such a job of bargaining that I got it for half the original price, and he was offered a job on the spot by the Jewish owner! This proved completely to me that here was the new Rockefeller, and I was certain I'd see his name soon in the financial columns. I was to meet him again, in Canada, in the most extraordinary circumstances.

My few months in Canada were about as undistinguished and nondescript as my university career. I was still just drifting, without plans or ambition. I had to work to eat, but the Depression was now really biting, and jobs were hard to come by. I worked for a while for General Motors in Oshawa, but then got laid off. My most lucrative and amusing job was working in a fun-fair in Toronto during the annual Jamboree, or whatever they called it, of the American Shriners. These are an order, like the Elks, who for some God knows reason, dress up as Egyptians or Turks or stage eunuchs. About 100,000 of them descended on Toronto, full of money and booze—that's why they came to Canada—and they were about the most ridiculous and stupid bunch of yahoos possible to imagine. The genius who employed me had produced an ordinary walking-stick, with, attached to the handle, one of those little pip-pip bulb horns that kids have on their bicycles. They caught on with the Shriners and we sold them by the thousand, at about twenty times their cost. The sight of a fat, middle-aged Yank, dressed in a red fez and a beer-stained burnous, creeping up on a pretty girl and then pip-pipping her bottom as the height of wit and

18

gallantry, was unforgettably nauseating. But at least what I made out of the bastards kept me for quite a while.

I was thinking of drifting out West and getting a job on the harvest, which was just starting, when I began to get disturbing letters from my mother. She was alone, wasn't well, nothing more to live for—very different from her usual independent attitude. I decided to go home.

I got to Montreal pretty broke. I hoped to work my passage home on a cattle-boat. All successful Canadians in Europe seemed to claim they had arrived on a cattle-boat. I found, to my considerable dismay, that it wasn't the cattle-boat season. (I had better explain that, in those days, cattle were brought over alive from Canada, in the holds of old freighters, and, for the privilege of mucking them out and feeding them for a couple of weeks, you got a free passage to Europe.) I was offered a berth to Greece, but I thought there were better places to be broke in than Athens. So I decided I'd have to pay my way. The cheapest fare was steerage on a CPR liner. But I hadn't got it. So it meant another job, and the Depression was worse. The trick was—and I perfected it in London later—to get the first editions of the papers as they came off the presses, and then walk —or run—to where the jobs were advertised.

I spotted a 'Commissionaire for Cinema Wanted' and was off like a shot. I was a bit late finding the cinema, but it was still, of course, closed. I made my way round the back, where I imagined the staff entrance would be. As I got into the sordid alley—which even the most magnificent cinemas always seem to back onto—I got a shock. There was a queue of men, at least a hundred yards long! I was just going to chuck it, but, in my conceit, I thought maybe I'd have a look at the kind of blokes who were waiting—perhaps I'd fit the uniform better. I strolled up the line, and they were a pretty scruffy bunch. And then, suddenly, there was my go-getter from St John's! In rags, and with about four days' beard on him. He spotted me, and grabbed my arm. He'd obviously been on the booze, as he had the shakes. All his dreams had come unstuck, the Depression had beaten him, as it was beating millions all over the world.

I was broke too, so I gave him a feed and lost him. But I felt a heel doing it.

Eventually, I got a job as a temporary wine waiter in a posh club. In a week, by saving my tips, and living at the YMCA, I had enough, with what I'd already got, to pay my fare—with one pound to spare. I kept that alive in a poker game most of the way across, but eventually landed at Greenock with half a crown. 'Go West, young man' hadn't done me much good.

* * * * *

My mother was, of course, delighted to see me. I found she had exaggerated a bit to get me back. She did get terrible migraines occasionally, but was well occupied with church work and her garden. I hung around for a while, enjoying the regular meals. But I knew it couldn't last. Although still lost, I felt I had to do *something*, and was pretty shaken by what I'd seen of the Depression at work. And I had no-one to ask for advice. My mother had divorced herself for so long from my father's public friends, that our only circle was in the little Argyllshire town of Dunoon, with its posher suburbs, Kirn and Hunter's Quay. So I turned to the family solicitor, a decent, but unworldly Highlander, called Callum MacPherson. His knowledge was mostly of hill farmers and boarding-house keepers, but he did tell me of a go-ahead Scotsman, Major Green, whom he'd met and been impressed with and who seemed to be going to do big things in London. He'd write him about me. He also told me that certain shares my father had made over to me some time before, their income being in lieu of an allowance, were worth £3,000. This was a real surprise. I was a capitalist. Like all theoretical Socialists who acquire money, I had no sudden inclination to give it away or embark on good works. I just stashed it away and thought about it. A certain Scots canniness, no doubt inherited from my father, kept me from blowing it. (After the split in the Liberal Party when Lloyd George was handing out titles like Green Shield stamps, he offered my father, a staunch Asquithian, a baronetcy. When my father told me he'd refused it—he did it on principle, of course—he added, with his wonderful twinkle 'What the hell do we want to be baronets for? Everything would cost double!' His loyalty to Asquith cost him his political career. He was chucked out, and, although he fought several more elections, never got back.)

Major Green wrote back that he would be pleased to take me on as a junior member of his organization, and so, in a new suit, and with the promise of my mother's daily prayers, I set off to breach the metropolis. (My mother had complete faith in the power of prayer. When we lived in Edinburgh, she developed a horrible rash on her neck, which started to spread upwards. She was a beautiful woman, and, naturally, the possibility of the rash covering her face was terrifying. In Edinburgh we had the advantage of one of the finest medical schools in the world. Specialist after specialist failed to halt the rash. Then my mother met a friend, who was a member of some obscure religious sect, who asked her if she would consider the use of prayer to cure her. My mother agreed, and that Sunday attended a meeting in some back-street tabernacle. When the service was over, the preacher asked 'Is there anyone here who is suffering from any affliction, who would like to be prayed for?' My mother, shaking with nervousness, stood up and said 'Yes, I have a skin disease.' The preacher asked her to come forward, and, putting his hands on her shoulders, made a powerful but straightforward appeal to God to cure her. Within a week the rash had gone.

I searched out Major Green's offices in London. Somehow, from the way Callum MacPherson had talked, I expected commissionaires, lifts, and, with luck, accessible secretaries. I was considerably shaken to climb a dingy staircase in an alley off Oxford Street, and wander into an almost furnitureless room, cluttered with packing-cases and cartons, amongst which a tiny gnome of a foreigner with a deformed hand was rummaging, helped by a ginger-headed Bessie Bunter who turned out to be his daughter. They told me that Major Green would be along presently, so, after hanging about for a bit, I waited at the entrance, to watch the bustle of the great city pass me by. I was joined there by a pimply youth, who seemed to be the only other member of the staff. Presently he nudged me, and said 'Here's the boss'. Coming towards us was a tall distinguished-looking figure, dressed in the height of City fashion, black jacket and striped trousers, light waistcoat, rose-bud in buttonhole, and topped off with a really magnificent Anthony Eden hat. His face was cadaverous and thin-lipped, but he had fine, shrewd piercing eyes. He spotted me and came forward with his hand out. 'You'll be Watt.' He then went on to say how glad he was I was joining him: what great things we'd do together. And during this speech I got my second shock of the morning. From his appearance, I had expected the clipped public-school drawl of the City boardroom. What I got was pure Glasgow Gorbals, the thick almost incomprehensible throat-muttering that you hear on a tram in Sauchiehall Street.

Major Green was a wonderful character. Brought up in the slums of Glasgow where, it was said, he had pushed a fish barrow, he went to the war with a Scottish regiment, and, having lived with and by fish all his life, was surprised to find that no fish of any kind was being served to the Army. He suggested to someone or other that perhaps he could get hold of some, and was told 'to get on with it'. He was apparently very successful —it is doubtful if any of his results reached the soldiers, but, no doubt, HQ were delighted to have sole or salmon for lunch before ordering a few more thousands of men to their deaths. So pleased were they that they made Green a Major, and he became known far and wide as 'The Fishmonger General'. When peace came, he used his majority to branch out as what he called a promoter, and lived precariously by his wits, generally teetering on the verge of bankruptcy. He was bursting with ideas and was a tremendous worker, and, I imagine, if he hadn't been fighting the Depression and the still class-ridden society of big business, could have been very successful.

He had just come back from America, and was determined to launch on Britain various money-making ideas he had spotted over there. The first three were to be midget-golf courses, chewing gum, and ice. Apparently—I had never even heard of it—midget-golf was sweeping America, and in every small township people were queuing up to pay for the privilege of putting a golf ball through a stucco lion's mouth, or over a miniature pagoda bridge. All you needed was to rent a vacant lot—of which there were plenty—put down a zig-zag tarmac channel, stick up some obstacles like old tyres or drainpipes, erect a pay kiosk, and bob's your uncle, the money would roll in. And since chewing gum was not generally used here in those days, but imported, the Major was going to launch a British chewing-gum company, with its own factory, and a massive countrywide sales campaign. He'd also noticed how every pub or sleazy café used ice in America, and he had decided to make Britain ice-conscious.

The tragedy was that all the ideas were tip-top, although he never got them very far off the ground. Midget-golf did proliferate throughout the country, but fizzled out as it did in America. Chewing gum must be an immense business all over Europe now—it is sad to see even the pretty young Spanish girls chewing with wide open mouths—and, before fridges and deep freeze, ice became more and more in demand.

All this he told me at a pub lunch on that first day. But his real interest, his whole enormous ambition, was concentrated on his boy Hughie. He was a genius, he was going on the stage, and he would be a star. Well, he did become a star—of a sort. He is Hughie Green, the host, I think they call it, of ITV's 'Opportunity Knocks'. He now looks like a tatty version of his father, but he hasn't got his charm. I think I was to get four quid a week to help launch this empire, but, as I seldom got paid, I've forgotten exactly.

But I will always remember 'The Fishmonger General' with the greatest affection.

My first job was helping Fritz Frieg—the little German I'd met in the storeroom-cum-office on my first day—construct and open a midget-golf course in Slough. As money was seldom forthcoming, we mostly did it ourselves, with the help of Bessie Bunter, and Frieg's unexpected wife, a plump, very pukka Englishwoman, of the type one expects to find in the bridge club of a suburban town. Frieg had been an engineer in Germany, where they had obviously been rather well-to-do.

We finished our course, with lots of ingenious hazards and bunkers, and waited for the money to pour in. For a time it did, and we got paid. But then other courses opened up in better situations and we began to see the writing on the wall. (I was seconded, for a while, to another of the Major's bright ideas. He brought over from America—I wonder if he ever paid for it?—the first Links Trainer, an ingenious machine that simulated, in a most realistic way, the control of an aeroplane. You sat in the cockpit, with an artificial horizon in front of you, and manipulated the joystick so that the machine turned, banked, dived and so on, exactly as a real plane would do. He had persuaded Selfridges to set it up in their store, and after a couple of rudimentary lessons, I was put in charge of it. I did the patter, demonstrated it, and took the money. Unfortunately, he asked a shilling a time, a considerable sum in those days, and it often broke down, so after about a fortnight Selfridges asked us to take it away. The Major was again away ahead of his time, as I understand sophisticated versions of this machine are used to this day to train air-crews.)

On my return to the midget-golf at Slough I found things were bad. One of our main sources of income had been boys from Eton College, but, inexplicably, our course was suddenly put out of bounds. It could not have been because of the tempting charms of Frieg's amiable but obese daughter, nor had we thought of selling illicit fags on the side. I can only imagine that their authority had decided that putting scruffy balls up drainpipes was *infra dig* for the future administrators of the nation. We weren't bringing in enough money even to fiddle our salaries. So something had to be done. It was now that Frieg produced his great scheme.

Somewhere, in his wanderings, he had met an Italian who claimed to have a revolutionary method of adapting standard leather machinery, designed to work on hides and skins, to operate on rubber. And the rubber it would work with, and produce beautiful even flat sheets, would be old inner tubes! From these, all sorts of products could be made, soles for sandals, beach balls, sealing rings for pickle bottles, and so on. Frieg obviously suspected that I had some cash stashed away, and when I let it out, it didn't take him long to persuade me to launch forth as a businessman. So The Hercules Rubber Co. Ltd. was formed. (It was an unfortunate name, as everyone thought we were making French letters, and must be coining money.) In fact, it was my biggest disaster.

Whenever I told the story of my one and only attempt to be an operative capitalist, my friends used to think it was hysterically funny; but looking back now, I can see it was a tragedy for so many people associated with it, Frieg and his nice family, the solid Midland engineer whom we took on as charge-hand, and the Scots salesman, desperately trying to defend his heavily mortgaged house in Stevenage. I was young enough, and irresponsible enough, and resilient enough to bounce back somehow, but to these people, our sordid little enterprise was a last chance to save them and theirs from the abyss that was opening in front of them, along with two million others.

The enormous mistake we made was that we all went into it

with such enthusiasm—and my three thousand quid. If only we'd decided to live for a year on the juice of an oily rag—and that would have been no change—experimented our process in some garden shed and then branched forth, I still think I'd have been a tycoon. As it was, we rented a bay in Slough Trading Estate, bought a lot of machinery, a few tons of inner tubes— aeroplanes' were best—and went into production.

The process was no swindle. Everything worked—up to a point. Inner tubes are made in different thicknesses all the way round, to stand different strains. When cut up by us into long rectangles and fed through our machines they came out beautiful flat sheets of the finest rubber, even in thickness to a millimetre. We decided our first main product would be beach balls, as we wanted a quick return from summer sales.

The method of making balls out of these sheets was most ingenious, and, I think, is worth describing. We stamped out of them a series of fat figures-of-eight shapes. By fat I mean with a thick waist. Onto every second flat eight we stuck a small square—about the size of a sugar cube—of pure crêpe rubber. Then the two figures of eight, which by their shape were complementary, were vulcanized together so that they became a strange flabby object with flat sides and rounded ends, about the size of a large grapefruit. A hypodermic needle was inserted from the outside through the little piece of crêpe rubber and compressed air pumped in. The strains were so calculated that, at a certain size, the 'thing' became perfectly round. By this time it had become a bit bigger than a football. When the needle was withdrawn, the cube of natural rubber inside sealed itself, and you had your ball. A quick spray with a few primary colours, and bingo, they were the best on the market, and half the price! You must remember that plastic balls did not exist, and the usual kids' ball, made of the poorest regenerated rubber, would hardly bounce. Ours were light, they bounced to the roof, and they were strong.

Our product sold like hot cakes! We bought more machinery on tick, had special cartons printed, and Frieg and George, the charge-hand-cum-head-mechanic, seemed to work twenty-four hours a day getting a proper production line operating. We had thirty girls—mostly Welsh—singing at their work, when the awful blow fell.

A large sack arrived from Southend, or somewhere like that. When we emptied it out onto the factory floor, it looked like a pile of the shrunken heads Amazonian Indians collect. They were our balls!—returned from their pristine rotundity to being 'things' again. The air had escaped! It was the vulcanizing. Apparently over a long period in storage, imperceptibly but inevitably, our balls leaked. Then came the deluge. By train, by carrier, by post, thousands of the pathetic shrunken little heads descended on us.

We stopped production, fired the sweet girls, and set out to find the trouble. We solved it, but it needed new equipment. And by now we were broke. We were depending on the returns from our sales to keep us going. Six pairs of frightened anxious eyes turned to me. I was the money man. But I knew nobody, so I wrote to my Highland friend, Callum MacPherson. The only person he knew with money, real money, was, of all people, Harry Lauder, who lived in Dunoon. He graciously agreed to discuss the matter. So Jock, our salesman, and I set off, in my bull-nosed Morris, to see what we could prise out of Harry Lauder's sporran. We were desperate. I remember that, the moment we crossed into Scotland at Gretna Green, we stopped the car, got out and silently gazed across our country-side. I am sure we were both putting up some sort of blasphemous Scottish prayer.

We were asked to dinner at Lauder Hall, the pretentious name for a pretty ordinary villa. Harry himself came to the door to meet us. He was an ugly, vulgar little man with the spurious joviality of the stage comedian. He led us inside, and, after a meagre drink, gave us one of the worst dinners I have ever eaten. He entertained us with interminable reminiscences of his interminable farewell tours. He at length allowed us to state our case. We reckoned a thousand or two would see us through, and genuinely believed it was a worthwhile invest-ment. Our host retired into another room with MacPherson and we made desultory conversation with Harry Lauder's niece, Greta, a handsome young woman whom he conned into being his general helper and dog's body for about thirty years, while waiting for his promised money.

Callum came back looking rather self-conscious and said 'Harry feels he has too many commitments at the moment to

26

consider . . .' He trailed off, because he knew the old bugger was rolling, and what some gesture would have meant to us. It was too late even to get drunk.

We got back to Slough to find our factory under siege. With the disappearance of our labour force, the buzz had gone round the local creditors, and they were arriving in droves. The only way we could see to get ready cash was to produce some saleable goods quickly. So we locked the doors and painted the windows, and the Friegs, Jock, George the fitter and I worked night and day for a fortnight, and turned out some excellent stuff. But it was too late. We were made bankrupt, and that was that.

I wasn't taken for a ride. The process, at that time, was, in a small way, a viable one. And the endeavour, initiative, mechanical ingenuity and sheer pluck shown by everyone, particularly Frieg, was a proud thing to remember.

*　　*　　*　　*　　*

I returned to London broke, but really broke. I'd had to sell everything, and then skip my digs. Yet the next few months were to be some of the most valuable of my life, because I got to know the poor. That's a patronizing phrase if ever there was one, and smacks of every liberal do-gooder, but, you see, I was a middle-class boy, brought up in security, and still with a mother who would send me a fiver if I asked for it. For someone like that to really understand what it is like—deep down—to live just to eat, and to eat be forced, for generations, into monotonous dead-end labour, with the chance of escape tens of thousands to one, is almost impossible. Pudovkin, the famous Russian film-maker, said the same. Himself a bourgeois, he spent his creative life portraying the workers. Although he succeeded brilliantly, he admitted that he himself could never get really inside them. It was something that worried George Orwell too, all his writing days. I daresay people will say this is old-hat, tub-thumping stuff. I admit I am writing and thinking of the early thirties. But there is still an awful lot of poverty about, and more and more monotony. I wonder how many Labour politicians, Union leaders, priests with their aura and their uniform, the boys who write in the *New Statesman* and *Tribune*, or the breast-beaters on television, know what it is really like to work on a conveyor belt in mass production, down a mine, or in a blast furnace? They've slipped up the smart way, and now carefully cultivate their working-class accents, whilst, I am sure, being half-ashamed of their parents.

I got a job with a rubber company that we had had dealings with. Its factory was an ancient warehouse in Cable Street, in the East End, bitterly cold and damp, employing about half a dozen hands. My work was pulling rubber sheets out of a machine, which constantly poured lubricating soapy water. I think we were given boots, but no protective clothing, and were generally soaked by the end of the day. My opposite number, who fed the sheets in, was Jack, a shining light in my memories. He was a good-looking, sharp-faced man of about thirty, with a shock of ginger hair, a grin that lit him up, and a thick Yorkshire accent. He came from a line of craftsmen who had, as far back as the family could remember, been the fitters, the installers, the maintainers of the machines in the mills that contributed so much to the wealth of Britain. His ancestors may have been around when the spinning jenny and the automatic looms were first installed, and, no doubt, got attacked by the other workers for their pains. And here was Jack, with his great and inherent skills, feeding rubber sheets through a messy machine for two pounds ten shillings a week. (Lots of people, when I've been yarning like this, have been frankly incredulous about the wages I have mentioned. I can only affirm that they are all accurate, and remind them, that, *in 1937*, the average miner earned between two and three pounds a week.)

The mills were shut, and their dead eyes looked out over the dead countryside. Jack, not wanting to die, brought himself and his little family to London, where the streets were paved with gold. They lived, of course, in one room, his bright boy and girl, and his sonsy wife, already beginning to look careworn. They shared an outside privy with innumerable others, and cleaned themselves once a week in the tin bath.

But Jack was a capitalist. He had an asset! He owned a good blue Sunday suit. And on Friday—we were paid on Saturday —that suit was pawned for ten shillings. It just kept the family going until the pathetic pay-envelope was handed over. Yet, regularly, on Saturday night, that suit was redeemed—with sixpence interest. Not to go to church—he wasn't stupid, he

28

knew that much of the slum property belonged to the Church Commissioners—but to take his little brood 'up West'. Threepence on the bus, and there were the bright lights, the nobs, the cinemas and theatres, the restaurants, the flash guys and the lucky. Then home, put away the suit, and bread and dripping.

It took a long time to find out all this about Jack, and be accepted into his spotless little home, and I had to box very cagey. One hint, one slip that you came from a different milieu, that although your values were the same, you had started it from a different level, and a sudden wall arose that was almost impossible to break down. I think this still applies today—if you don't agree, try starting an intellectual argument in your local public bar. So many of my highbrow associates think they can 'meet the working man'. Malcolm Muggeridge, for instance, my revered and close friend. He hasn't a hope. There's that ghastly accent to start with. (I wonder if I would have talked like him if I'd gone to Cambridge, as my father suggested?) And he's incapable of meandering on with the platitudes, repetitions and sudden flashes of colour in ordinary man's speech. Without an innocuous Scots accent, a knowledge of football, boxing, cricket and horse racing, plus a few dirty stories mostly involving the bosses, and a capacity to swear, without repeating myself, for about two minutes, I could never have found the material to write the documentary films I did, both in peace and war. I imagine that Malcolm, master of words that he is, has not got these gifts. I once went with him to see *The Bridge Over The River Kwai* in a suburban cinema in Sydney, Australia. It was not one of my happier evenings. To start with, Malcolm can never speak *sotto voce*. He declaims, wherever he is. And that exaggerated 'Pommy' voice, echoing out over the Bijou Cinema, Cronulla, nearly started a riot. When William Holden, the co-star, disappeared, apparently killed, Malcolm said—as usual, at the top of his voice—'Thank God that dreary Yank has gone. I found him intolerable!' I explained, very *sotto voce*, that Holden had been paid a million dollars for the picture, and as it was only a third of the way through, he was bound to reappear. When he did, Malcolm boomed 'How clever you are, Harry, I can never understand the economic intricacies of your dreadful industry. So we have to put up with the awful shit to the end.' At that, an enormous Rugby League forward, sitting behind us, got up and said 'Listen, you Pommy poof, one more word out of you, and I'll sink ya.' Malcolm, of course, was not in the least discountenanced, and merely said, very mildly, 'My dear chap, I was only making what I thought was a perfectly valid criticism of a rather second-rate piece of cinema.' The gorilla sat down, baffled. But I imagine Malcolm would have had great difficulty in achieving an intimacy with that Aussie.

Gradually, I got to know the rest of the gang. There was the young Cockney humper whose vivid descriptions of the factory, and our employers, their sexual perversions and aberrations, helped to keep us alive. He was constantly bemoaning the loss of his last job, packing 'fanny wrappers', or sanitary towels. He was able to pinch quite a lot, and had considerable success with the local girls handing them round. He carefully explained what a relief it was, in those days before the pill, when your girl-friend asked you to pinch a packet for her.

Then there was The Dandy, a tall, flashily handsome young man, whose sensuous joy on a Saturday was to go to the barber and have the works: shave, trim, shampoo, face massage and, crowning luxury, have his blackheads squeezed out. And then, with his skinny little bird, 'Up West', this time not to look at the pigeons or the buildings, but to stroll around the best places, imagining that the passers-by imagined you were on your way to Romano's or The Hungaria for a cocktail. I have such a vivid memory of him telling me about it on the Monday morning. 'You oughtta seen me, 'Arry. The old 'at like this'—a graphic gesture with his hands, and there was his curly-brimmed bowler over one eye—'and the tie out 'ere, and the pin just so, and the 'andkerchief just showing—matching, mind yer. And the strides. 'Arry, you could 'ave cut your bleeding fingers on the crease. It's an old army lurk me Dad give me, soap inside, along the creases, see, and then me Mum irons them. Cut your bloody fingers, you could. And me shoes, 'Arry boy, me new shoes'—he points his long, sensitive and quite filthy fingers in front of him —'like needles they are, fuckin' needles'. He waits for my expressions of awe, and then says 'We didn't 'half 'ave a good time. I seen people looking at us.' He made me want to cry, of course, because his simple joys were those of my father. Only nobody whispered as he passed.

Then our tiny corner of capitalism collapsed. I was happy

that they found another job for Jack, where his skills could be used, but the rest of us were out.

I answered one of those flash advertisements that one still sees: 'Smart, educated young men wanted by progressive firm to train as executives, etc. etc.' I knew they usually ended up as selling tatty encyclopaedias or silk stockings from door to door, but what the hell? I might screw them for something before it became intolerable. It turned out to be British Home Stores, then just starting up in this country, and run, to my surprise, by the Neisner Chain Store Corporation, of Chicago. They gave me the inevitable vast forms to fill in and, by means of stressing my background and skimming over my present, I seemed to qualify, because I was summoned before a panel of grey-faced pomposities and lectured on the marvellous opportunity that was opening up in front of me. However, every Carnegie had to start at the bottom, learn the business, move through the departments, in order to ... and so on. They no doubt used 'shoulders to the wheel, hands to the pumps, best foot forward' but I wasn't listening any more. All I was wondering was what it would pay. And, would you believe it, it was three quid a week! I was to become a storeman at their most recent and up-to-date establishment, in Kilburn High Street. It's still there, and every time I pass it, I spit.

When I gratefully accepted their kind and generous offer, the head man gave me another interminable homily, and then they all stood up, shook my hand and wished me luck, as though I was setting off for the North Pole. Why are Americans so bloody serious about business? I remember, years later, at Ealing Studios, all the directors were notified that the head of the American Censorship Board, or whatever his title was, intended to come for lunch, and we were invited to meet him. He turned out to be a ghastly old bore, but, as we were getting a free lunch, we put up with him until, towards the end, he suddenly said 'Gentlemen, I have something to tell you that is going to worry you very much. It will do more than worry you, it will shock you.' We all stopped eating and waited. Christ, were the Yanks going to ban British films? Or put on a prohibitive tax? The old ham savoured the dramatic pause, and then went on 'Gentlemen, the Women's Clubs of America are getting stronger!' It became the best gag we'd had for weeks in the pub across the road. 'I'm going to worry you, in fact, I'm going to shock you—it's your round.'

I duly reported to Kilburn High Street, and there began the most horrific experience of my somewhat bizarre youth. The Neisner Corporation were onto a good thing. Unlimited unorganized labour, and a growing demand for the cheapest goods. They had slotted themselves neatly between Woolworths and Marks & Spencers, so had an enormous range of articles. This was where I came in. I didn't realize—and I imagine many people don't today—that the turnover in such stores is such that they need about as much storage space as they have floor space. Thus, at Kilburn, the whole of the first floor above the selling area was a vast maze of racks, shelves, bins and so on, filled with about ten times the amount of merchandise as was on display below. At the end of this storage area, there was a large bare reception room, linked to the alley at the back by a service lift. It was my job, helped by one other sucker—the first one was the son of an undertaker from Newcastle—to load into the lift the constant stream of packing cases, cartons, crates, etc. brought by lorry, unload them at the top, open them, check them, count, and then pack the contents into their appropriate shelves. But—and this was hell—we had to bring to the front all goods already on the shelves so that they would be sold first, and put our new stuff behind it. We had then to make good all containers that were returnable, get them down into the alley, and make out reports on damage or breakages. (There was a 5 per cent permissible breakage allowance on glass and crockery, so we had orders to smash some perfectly good plates or glasses if there had been no damage in transit, to be kept in a bucket as proof of the claim, should there be a query.)

By the time we'd more or less finished these jobs, the requisition chits began to come up from the main floor. These were forms filled in by the young girl counter-hands, stating what they needed to renew their stocks. In fact, roughly what they had sold that day. We storemen had to collect these goods from the racks and shelves, and pile them into large wicker baskets. That sounds reasonably simple, but when they ranged from a gross of handkerchiefs to four teapots, ten mechanical toys, two bottles of boiled sweets, seventy pairs of stockings, and on and on through hundreds of articles, it was a lot of finicky work, particularly—and this really got us down—as we had to immediately rearrange the shelves in perfect symmetry wherever we had removed anything.

We then carried the full baskets down the stairs to the main floor—I'm getting tired just writing this—and distributed the goods to the appropriate counters. There were usually balls-ups, as the little dears were no scholars. We again tidied upstairs and it was time to close. Then the storemen swept out the shop! Seventy hours a week to climb the ladder with good old Neisner —if you lived!

The treatment of the girl assistants was equally bad. Because at least half a dozen young women from the industrial north and Wales came in each day looking for work, British Home Stores, of course, took advantage of this, and paid their counter-hands eighteen shillings and sixpence a week. I can't imagine why some did not turn to prostitution. American methods were still being applied, and all of us had to stagger in at half-past eight. Then—and if you put this scene in a film about a prison camp, you'd hardly believe it—we were forced to gather at the music counter, and stand there, half-starved and shivering, while an elderly lady thumped out the latest hits on an out-of-tune piano, and we sang! 'I Want To Be Happy'—oh God! It was to put us in a cheerful mood for our tasks. Then the manager harangued us on our sales records in comparison with other stores: 'Harlesden was having a terrific run with bras-sières, and Neasden, with a special display, had almost sold out that new line in lipsticks, but he was glad to see . . .' He was a decent, horribly harassed young man, and I think he knew that nobody was listening. We then dispersed joyfully to our various labours, with a song in our hearts, or so Chicago thought.

By law, the girls had to be provided with a stool behind the counter, to sit on in slack periods. They were instantly dismissed if they were seen using them.

The terror of the whole store were the unheralded visits of the chain's inspector, a hard-faced American called Simons. I sup-pose he thought he was instilling current United States business methods into the decadent British, but, in fact, he was a sadistic bully. Having frightened half the girls into tears, he'd swoop on our department. He would march along the shelves like a sergeant-major inspecting the kits of a delinquent platoon, followed by the manager—who always developed a twitch when Simons was around—and me and my mate, registering dumb hate. When he found anything wrong with the arranging, he'd pull it all out onto the floor, stick a couple of things back as he wanted it, and leave us to clear up the mess. He loved to demonstrate his efficiency by spotting small details. One hot day he saw half a dozen of the large glass jars of boiled sweets standing in the reception room. With the heat, half the sweets had melted into a solid lump, and they'd been sent up from the floor as unsaleable. Simons pounced on them with 'There's your praafit, there's your praafit. Loosen them up, and send them down again'. What the bastard didn't realize was that there was a large returnable charge on the bottles and in trying to prise the bloody sweets out with a long-handled screwdriver, I broke about two quids' worth of bottles. I must admit I wasn't applying the delicate touch of a brain surgeon.

The climax arrived one Wednesday afternoon during a Simons visit. Suddenly, as he raged at some petty fault in the packing, I'd had enough. I didn't lose my temper—then. I just said 'That's it', walked to the door and put my jacket on. As I started for the stairs, the manager ran after me and said, 'Oh, for Christ's sake, Harry, forget it. We all know what a bastard he is. But you've stuck it so long, hang on now.' As I said, I liked him, and had seen him humiliated often enough by Simons, so I relented and went back to work.

On the Saturday, with my pay packet, were my cards. I'd been fired! I rushed to the manager with the time-worn question 'What's this, then?' He explained that Simons had sent him after me with instructions to butter me up to stay on until a substitute could be found, and then fire me. Now I lost my temper. Fortuitously, I had been unpacking large brown china teapots. They threw beautifully. 'Fuck Simons' took the first against the wall with a wonderful thwack and satisfactory disintegration. 'Fuck British Home Stores' and 'Fuck Yanks' followed the next two. My mate put his head through the door: 'Fuck you' accompanied the teapot aimed at him. 'And fuck you too' took another as the manager appeared and disappeared at the top of the stairs. I went through my repertoire again, and the floor began to look like an Aunt Sally stall after a busy weekend. Then I walked out.

34

To his credit, the manager didn't tell the police. But I bet British Home Stores had a large claim in for teapots damaged in transit.

So what to do, what to do, as the Indian stationmaster said when he saw two trains approaching from opposite directions on the same line. I had tried hard at Kilburn, and six other blokes had come and gone during my stint there. But I did now want to show something a bit more solid for my efforts because I had met the girl I eventually married, who I imagined was somewhat embarrassed that her boy-friend's only social asset was making people laugh about his misfortunes. She had a considerable influence on me, because she stopped me taking a job with Bertram Mills Circus, which showed I was settling down.

I was nursing a coffee in Soho—we had the Spanish capacity to sit on one drink all day—when someone mentioned that a Scotsman, called, he thought, John Grierson, was starting up a film company in Oxford Street and there just might be jobs going. The Scots are like the Jews, they have relations everywhere, and the name struck a faint bell. So I wrote to a cousin, who telephoned his cousin, and I eventually got a letter of introduction to Grierson. With no optimism at all, I made the appointment to see him.

*　　*　　*　　*　　*

The grey-faced man scribbling hieroglyphics into a notebook on the big desk—it turned out to be his almost indecipherable writing—flung down his pen, swung round towards me and said 'Tell me about yourself.' I was intimidated. The eyes were piercing and bored into you. There was a tremendous feeling of suppressed energy, almost of fanaticism. John Grierson, trained for the Scottish Church, had had his vision. The vision of forming a unit to make films called 'documentary', about the real people and the real happenings that were taking place around us, as distinct from the synthetic snobbish imaginings of second-rate writers, that were the British films of the early thirties.

I stumbled into most of what I have recounted here. Although some of the episodes made good pub yarns, they sounded pretty sordid and unconvincing when you were applying for a job. With those sharp eyes on me, it never occurred to me to tell anything but the truth. When I didn't even get a smile after the story of the rubber balls, I thought 'Oh Christ' but swallowed and ploughed on. I knew Grierson must be thinking 'Why should I give this kid a job, just because he's Scots, and has a letter from a mutual friend?' I dried up, and his eyes flickered back to the notebook. Then, in desperation, I said 'Two years ago, I sailed the Atlantic.' There was a sudden change. Grierson jumped from his chair, strode to the window and said 'Tell me about it.' (I found out later that Grierson—in the office at any rate—never walked. He strode, leapt, rushed, banged and crashed, but never walked.)

I sat and told him the whole story of the voyage of the *Neptune*. Grierson stared out of the window, only grunting a few sharp questions, and waving away his faithful factotum Golightly whenever he put his anxious head around the door. When I had finished, there was a long silence, as Grierson stayed staring out of the window. What I did not know then was that he was mad about the sea, and no doubt he was imagining the old schooner as she rose to the westerly swell, and the rush of activity when the skipper shouted 'Stand by to go about'. Suddenly he was back in his chair, scribbling something. He swung towards me and said 'You'd better start on Monday.' I was so astonished I only managed to mumble 'Thank you very much' and shuffle out.

At the right moment, utterly by chance, I had struck the right note. It is this sort of lucky break you always seem to need to get on in this crazy business.

Years later, Grierson, writing about the formation of The Empire Marketing Board Film Unit, which was the prosaic and uninspiring name for what I had joined, said 'Of the 1,500 tyros who applied for jobs in the EMB Film Unit, 1,500 exactly expressed their enthusiasm for cinema, for art, for self-expression, and the other beautiful what-nots of a youthful or simply vague existence.' You were wrong, Mr Grierson! You forgot Watt. He only wanted to eat.

2

I duly reported back on the Monday. The whole Unit's headquarters was a floor and a half in an old-fashioned block in
Oxford Street. I stuck my head into various doors, and either
saw individuals hidden behind vast amounts of film hung up in
strips over plastic bins, or stumbled on groups arguing fiercely
about almost any subject except cinema. No-one paid the
slightest attention to me.

I finally found Golightly, whom I remembered as having
something to do with Grierson. He was a slight, dapper, balding
man, whose rimless glasses and benign air gave him the
appearance of a private tutor to a well-to-do family. He kept
the books, handled the vague staff problems, and coped with
Grierson, to whom he was devoted. He told me to find Jimmy
Davidson, and left it at that. I finally found a large room, cluttered with tripods, very elderly cameras, tins of film, title cards
stuck on bits of board, and a jungle of lamps and wires. Its only
occupant was a thin, nervous man, sucking on a very long and
empty pipe, who gave the appearance that it was all too much,
and that at any moment he was going to smash something.
Certainly trying to make sense of the chaos that was around
him was a pretty formidable task. When I tentatively asked 'Mr
Davidson?' he snapped 'Yes, yes, what is it?' I said 'Mr
Grierson told me to report for work.' That stopped him in his
tracks. He took his pipe out of his mouth and said 'Oh Jesus,
not another one?' Neither Christ nor I answered, so we just
stood and looked at each other. Then he said 'What do you do?'
On my first day in a business of which I knew nothing, this was
rather a tricky question, particularly as it was obvious Davidson
thought I was a write-off from the start. I could see he wouldn't
be impressed if I said I played a pretty good game of midget-
golf. So I said nothing, and we continued to look at each other.
He glanced around desperately to break the impasse, and

suddenly seized a bucket. 'Can you whitewash?' I don't think I'd ever even painted anything, but this was no moment to quibble. I imagined you just mixed it, and sloshed it on. So I agreed, enthusiastically. In ten minutes my great creative moment had arrived. I had my bucket, a ladder, a brush, and a soupy white mess. I sloshed it on the wall, myself and the floor, and it all looked horribly streaky. Later in the day, I was helped by a little chap who came out of one of the cutting-rooms. He had been hired to do a cutting job for a couple of weeks, and he was waiting for more film material to come in. He turned out to be Sidney Cole, who became a top producer at Ealing Studios, and is still going strong with *Danger Man* and *Man with a Suitcase*. I am glad to report that his whitewashing was just as bad as mine.

There followed a frenetic and, in retrospect, hilarious year for me as an assistant director. In feature films, an assistant graduates from carrying tea and sticking up notices, through 'Ready on the set, Mr Niven', to trying to keep dreary extras enthusiastic after the twentieth take of the hero winning the Derby on a mechanical horse. In the EMB the assistant did pretty well everything. The cameramen were usually profes-sionals hired by the day. The director chose the shots and the camera set-ups. The assistant did the rest. I didn't mind hump-ing the gear, or getting permissions, or the Augean job of trying to stop passers-by looking at the camera, but it was the electrical side that petrified me. For some reason—and it has always irritated my womenfolk more than any of my vices—I am utterly clumsy with all things mechanical. Try to mend any-thing, and it's broken forever. Put up a shelf, and it falls down in a week. I loathe men who boast of their achievements around the house. I know their stupid yammerings are going to be used against me. So one can imagine my horror when I found I was supposed to be an electrician as well. I never learnt the first principles of electricity. I would lug our rather pathetic lights and rolls of cable out to some housing estate, and be immedi-ately baffled by a stream of technical gobbledegook from the house electrician! I'd try and persuade him to connect up his end, and then I had a go at our junction box. Almost inevitably there were clouds of smoke, horrible smells, and occasional flashes. I gave myself dreadful shocks, and ruined budgets with burst bulbs. It was when Golightly suddenly noticed the bill for bulbs, that I was relieved as 'Sparks', an appropriate name. But it was a black mark against me. Grierson expected everyone to be able to do anything, although we were never given any proper training. You just taught yourself by trial and error, and picking the brains of those who were decent enough to help you. What Grierson did do was to generate a tremendous enthusiasm, and a belief that what you were doing was unique. It was a strange set-up.

It had come about when Grierson returned from a scholarship stay in New York. Being a fine journalist, he got some film reviewing to do on the *New York Sun*. In one of his reviews he coined the word 'documentary' to represent a film of reality. It was really a direct translation of the French 'Documentaire', already in use. Some good realist films had been made in Berlin and Paris of a city at work or play, asleep or awake, but these had been sporadic individual efforts, often leaving the makers broke and bitter.

Somehow or other Grierson raised a few thousand quid in London, and made a film called *Drifters*, about the Scottish herring fleet. It was a really brave effort, as Grierson knew absolutely nothing about film-making. He was helped by a long-suffering team of professionals who, of course, thought the whole thing a waste of time. Then it was premiered at a Sunday showing of the London Film Society, which all the best critics always attended, and its impact was tremendous. Seeing it now, one is perhaps astonished. Though it used revolutionary Russian montage techniques it is slow and lacking in human warmth. After the tens of thousands of documentary films that have been poured out during the war, and now on TV, one can hardly believe that such an effort could have brought about so much. But one has got to try and realize that no-one had ever seen a real worn British working man's face on the screen, that no-one had ever watched a worker with hands like hams and fingers like sausages, lovingly mend a net with the skill and precision of an artist. And very few realized just how hard physical work was. The omnipotent middle class had their eyes and their social conscience opened up, just for a moment.

The *succès d'estime* of *Drifters* (it was too much to expect it to get many cinema showings) brought an offer to Grierson of more money to make another film. And here came his great stroke of genius. He said he'd use the money to form a Unit. Perhaps he realized when making *Drifters* that actual film-making was not his *métier*. He only made one other short film. But from his gesture, and because of his superb sense of propaganda and public relations in the widest sense, a new British art-form arose that led the world, and eventually influenced and changed the whole of our cinema.

His method of recruitment for the Unit was eccentric, as I think I have made clear. When I arrived, the seniors were Arthur Elton, Basil Wright, and Stuart Legg, all from the universities, who must have given Grierson that art talk that he wrote about. Their knowledge of the techniques of Eisenstein and Pudovkin awed me. Elton was a huge, bearded, Viking-like character, who dressed like a tramp. He was the heir to an ancient and impoverished baronetcy in the West Country, who had the right of sturgeon and swan in the Bristol Channel. A genius for describing the working of machines simply and graphically on film, he obviously disliked people. But he does have a credit on one little beauty, *Housing Problems*, which was years ahead of its time, and remains one of the most moving films about the bravery of poverty. (Actually made by John Taylor and Ruby Grierson, and produced by Elton.)

Basil Wright was a dark, intense ascetic, with a great deal of the poet in him. He made some beautiful films later on, including the classic *Song of Ceylon*, and was always kind and helpful to me. He had the misfortune to be rich, which I have always felt to be a drawback to a creative artist. Like hungry boxers are the best boxers.

Stuart Legg was brilliant, skilful and dull. Everything he did was utterly correct technically, and looked it. But he was a good aide to Grierson, in the interminable pumping out of the propaganda that kept us alive, and persuaded bewildered civil servants to continue our grants. It has always seemed to me that these writings and *pronunciamentos* on documentary, whether because of Grierson's Calvinism, or the fact that they were mostly aimed at the highbrow weeklies and quarterlies, were pretty boring. One of Legg's gems reads 'In the thirties British documentary opened up the themes of civics and civic reform and therefore established a position for itself in the leadership of national thinking'. Grierson constantly said the same sort of thing much better. To this day writers on British documentary make it sound like one of the more solemn research foundations. No-one ever seems to have recorded that we were just a bunch of enthusiastic kids, accepting the basic theme of the dignity of man from our brilliant but erratic boss, learning our job by trial and error, bubbling with ideas but making thousands of mistakes, cheerfully exploiting ourselves and each other in the absolute belief that what we did or were going to do was worthwhile. No-one has ever suggested that we were happy, that we laughed. And we had a million laughs.

The middle echelon of the hierarchy consisted of Edgar Anstey, now producer of the Transport Board Film Unit, a Canadian woman called Evelyn Spice—I never found out how she got into the act—Donald Taylor, a rather flash young man who would obviously have preferred to have been in feature films, and two sisters of Grierson, who, as it happens, were talented as well as charming girls. Until the arrival of Pat Jackson, I continued to be the lowest form of human life around.

Grierson had apparently been cornered by an eager beaver of a boy while lecturing at Bryanston School, and had weakened again to give him a job. He was lanky, pink-faced, frightfully willing, and very very pukka. What Jimmy Davidson's comment must have been when he rolled up, we hated to think. But he obviously decided to make the best of it, and promoted young Pat to be projectionist, one of the innumerable jobs Davidson did himself. I happened to be in the theatre for the rushes on Pat's first morning.

The ceremony of the rushes—that is, the viewing of the previous day's filming, developed but uncut as they came out of the camera—was quite a formal one. When the film had been checked and handed to the projectionist, Golightly was informed, who in turn told Grierson. Those of us involved in rushes that day sat and waited in the miniscule theatre. We'd hear Grierson's door being kicked open, the rush down the passage, the kick into the theatre, the crash into the front seat and the grunt 'Shoot'. We'd than tap on the projectionist's window—the buzzer never worked—and off we'd go.

Young Pat got his machine working all right, and even managed to rack the frame into the correct position. But after about two minutes, there was a horrible rasping noise from the projection booth, the picture on the screen disintegrated into a series of rather beautiful zigzag patterns, and then nothing. A very pink, sweating little face appeared through the door, and the immortal phrase fell on the awful silence 'I say, sir, I'm *damned* sorry.'

Pat Jackson went on to make the best war documentary, *Western Approaches*, and many other fine films.

There finally came the day, when through holidays or illness or something, I was suddenly ordered out to direct my first scenes. They were three shots, for a montage, of three different nationalities posting a letter. I was allotted as my cameraman George Noble, one of the real characters of early documentary. He wasn't documentary at all, of course, being just a daily free-lance professional, and he thought we were all nuts. But we represented a pretty steady three pounds a day. He was a short very fat Cockney, of magnificent ugliness. He wore, winter and summer, a dreadful plus-four suit with what seemed the stains of a lifetime spread across it. His immense belly oozed out over his belt—usually an old school tie—and his eyes bulged like poached eggs behind enormous pebble glasses. And yet he had more success with women than all of us quite personable youngsters rolled together. He laughed them into bed. He was a genuinely funny man, and I firmly believe women are much more likely to just give up and give in after a night of laughter than a night of repetitive sweet talk. George had no time for anything highbrow. He always said as we left the office 'Now, none of that arty-farty crap. Dead on and pin sharp, that's my motto.' He was tiptop at his job.

I had decided that an Italian, an Indian, and a typical Scandinavian would do for my shots. Because of our Spartan training, it never occurred to me that I could have got three such types for a few bob, searched out a quiet pillar-box, and faked everything at my leisure. No, we had to be real. So we headed straight for Soho. I went in and chatted up a pretty, very Italian looking waitress while George set up the camera beside the nearest, and busiest, pillar-box. Today, with TV units in every second street and commercials being shot beside practically every statue in London with hand-held 16mm cameras, and long-focus lenses with wider apertures than our 40mm lenses had, it all seems a piece of cake. But in 1932, a camera in the street was an event. Particularly as they were the immense old American jobs, the kind one used to see in publicity stills of Lubitsch or Capra. It wasn't out of the case before a crowd had gathered. And by the time it had been mounted on the clumsy giro tripod, and the 1,000-foot magazine fitted and threaded up, it was liable to stop the traffic.

The little Italian waitress was quite willing to help me. Every amateur who is asked to cooperate on a film is delighted, and everyone gets disillusioned in the process. By the time I got with her to George at the pillar-box, the crowd was quite thick. They were disappointed with my waitress, because most of them knew her, and had expected some sexy actress. I explained to my girl that she should come in from the left, pause for a moment to read the collection times, pop in the letter, and walk out to the right. She understood perfectly. I then had to get the crowd away. I went into the patter I'd used plenty of times for other directors (me, a director?): 'Look, we're taking a scene for a film, do you mind standing over here, behind the camera, you can watch as much as you like, of course, it's your pavement after all, ha ha—but we want to make it as natural as possible —we're trying to pretend the camera isn't here—and if you walk past, *please* don't look at the camera.' Christ, if I'd had a pound for every time I've said that, I'd be running a yacht in Monte Carlo! Most of the people were always pretty decent, and either just went, or shuffled behind the camera hoping something interesting would happen. But there was always the awkward bastard who said it was his pavement, it was his pillar-box. How I longed to tell him I'd shove it up his jacksy if he didn't move off. But I had to do the old diplomacy: 'I agree, of course, you have a perfect right to stand where you like, but we're just trying to do a job, like you do'—the prick obviously hadn't worked in twenty years—'and you've never seen anybody post a letter in somebody's flies, have you, ha ha!'—bloody little Algerian ponce—'so do you mind, sir?' And finally everything is clear, and I tell George to start the camera, and sign to the girl, and this is it, I'm in, I'm a director, Hollywood here I come! And the stupid little bitch walks up to the box, sticks the letter in, and turns to me with a lovely smile and says 'E buono?' So I say cut, and mean her throat, and all the frustrated directors in the crowd, who couldn't direct the vital shot in a dirty film, start telling her what she did wrong, and her boss wants her back because business is good, and we start again. And the next time she walks out the wrong way, and next time the sun goes out, and the next time she drops the letter, and the next time a drunk sticks his head in the camera, and the next time her brother walks into the shot, and the next time it's perfect. And I'm a director!

By now it's lunch time and the Indian cook I'd lined up for the second shot is too busy pouring curry powder over horse-meat to play with me. So George and I have beer and sand-wiches, while he regales me with the details of the women he's had in the last week. I'm not even jealous, because I'm dream-ing of a vast cosmopolitan crowd drifting casually past a pillar-box, while an Indian Rajah arrives in a palanquin and posts an enormous crested envelope.

About 2.30 I have to settle for Abdul, who looks like a Jewish bookie's runner. I finally get him to borrow a turban from a Sikh pal of his, and, to my utter surprise, the shot goes off with-out a hitch. There was hardly any colour problem in those days, and a coloured man posting a letter was just not interesting.

So now there's the Scandinavian. I go into a restaurant called 'Swedish Kitchen, Smorgesbord and open Sandwiches' and they all look Spanish to me. I think of playing the part myself—I was blond in those days—but funk the cracks back in the Unit. And suddenly the perfect type comes out of a book-shop. About six-foot-six, white-blond, every inch a Swedish seaman. He turns out to be a pork-butcher from Liverpool. I persuade him to take his jacket off, and he's the part. Writing to tell the folks back home the price of fish in England, and how he's longing to get back to his little Inga. Everything's set up, nobody's looking at the camera, so I say 'Roll 'em' and then 'Action'. The pork-butcher performs perfectly, and I turn to George to say 'OK?' and he's not there!

George was about fifty yards down the street, chatting up a very hot-looking piece of talent. I tore after him, and gave him about seventeen four-letter words. The girl didn't flinch, but just remarked primly to George, 'I don't like your friend.' George started to introduce me, when I cut him short by saying did he know his camera was unattended? Christ, in Soho? He did the fifty yards back in even time. Of course, Charlie the butcher was still there. The pubs were shut, and I had his jacket. Mumbling fearful indecencies about the bottom of the girl he'd lost, George shot the shot, and we packed up, and retired to a seedy drinking club, where George helped Charlie make some doubtful contacts, and I stood a round of doubles to celebrate my emergence from the shadows.

I lay awake most of the night going over and over those three dreary little scenes. Should I have changed the angles more for each shot? Should I have covered each one in close-up? Should I have chosen a different location for each? The permutations and combinations of three shots and one camera seemed infinite. I finally fell asleep convinced I'd chosen the wrong ones.

Next morning, I waited for the boy from Humphries Laboratories. My tiny contribution to posterity rattled pathetically in the big 1,000-foot tin. I made sure the leads were on properly, that it was wound round the right way, and handed it over to young Pat, with strict instructions to watch his rack.

Then I reported to Golightly and waited. Sitting there, I had the same uneasy, nervous feeling that I was to have every time I ran rushes for the next forty years. For that is the moment of truth. There are no more alibis. You may have compromised with sponsors, producers, budgets and the weather; you will have battled with blasé technicians, uncooperative actors, and the endless mechanical problems that constantly bedevil the translation of an idea into a moving piece of celluloid; you will certainly have expended an enormous amount of physical and nervous energy. But finally you will have said 'Cut and print', and then you are on your own. It is your decision, and yours alone. This incoherent jumble of shots, full of false starts, flashes and *non sequiturs*, is your painting, your song, your poem. You imagined them and you created them. And always, before they start, you are alone. I have waited, surrounded by helpers, in the Australian desert while they threaded up a dreadful clapped-out portable projector, or in Africa, seeing rushes that had been to Hollywood and back, or in the pseudo-baroque magnificence of a multi-million studio, and always, as I waited, I was terribly lonely. The moment they start you are a technician again, analysing, selecting, and advising the editor. But that emptiness in your belly will come back again.

After what seemed an interminable time, we went through the usual Grierson noise routine, and there it was on the screen. Not bad, not bad. The Italian girl looked real and pretty. Nice Soho atmosphere. Then Abdul. A bit phoney, maybe, but only I knew about the turban. And Charlie looked great. Straight up from the docks. And then, and then . . . Just as Charlie paused to peer at the collection times, with a really brilliant look of a dumb deck-hand, a small boy popped out of a doorway behind him, spotted us, and grinned right at the camera! Grierson was out of his seat like a shot.

'Did you see that bloody boy?'

'Yes.'

'Then why the hell didn't you re-shoot?'

'I didn't see him at the time.'

'Why not?'

'I was watching Charlie.'

'Who's Charlie?'

'The Swede.'

'Looked like an American to me.'

'Actually, he's from Liverpool.'

Awful pause.

'It's a bit difficult, you know, in Soho, the . . .'

'Christ, he was centre screen. I don't want your excuses. What do you think I pay you for?'

Which was a bit hard, as I was getting three quid a week. The interesting thing, looking back and remembering this scene, is how, cheerfully and with real affection, we took Grierson's autocratic bullying. We knew he was a perfectionist, and was doing his utmost to turn us into perfectionists. We also knew that he was protecting us, and enabling us to learn our trade, which we desperately wanted to do. For, basically, the EMB was a bunch of amateurs, and our films were generally pretty poor efforts, ballyhooed out of all proportion by Grierson's tireless writing and lecturing.

I went back to my assisting somewhat reluctantly, but with considerably more respect for the directors. After a while I was approached by Donald Taylor to help him. He had been commissioned to do a film called *Spring Comes to England* for the Ministry of Agriculture. When the word got around that a Government Department actually had a film unit, other departments started to want to have their photographs taken too. Because that was exactly their attitude. They knew nothing of Cinema, and were proud of the fact. What they wanted was a series of 'snaps', preferably of the chief Civil Servant, or even The Minister, getting out of an official car, and opening some dreary new project. It wasn't until I was much more senior that I fully grasped the incredible job Grierson had done in side-tracking these gruesome gnomes, and getting and keeping for us the freedom we needed. One moment's weakening, one moment's relaxing of the creative standards he was trying to imbue into us and into documentary, and we'd have been finished. It was never done by force, or stand-up rows. The Establishment was much too strong for that. It was done by sheer diplomacy, by persuading our sponsors that they were true patrons of the Arts, with exquisite taste, and then selling them the film—which usually they couldn't understand—so hard they had accepted it before they had time to think. After-wards, it was fairly easy to get a few highbrow critics to give you a write up, send the clips to the sponsor, and in a week he was going around saying 'Have you seen my film?' Grierson was helped greatly by Sir Stephen Tallents, the sensitive and highly intelligent head of the Empire Marketing Board, who was per-haps the only official who understood what Grierson was after. It was he who saved our lives later on, when it looked as though we were all for the high jump.

Tallents also protected us from the inevitable slurs that began to be bruited round Whitehall that we were 'a gang of Bol-sheviks'. We were neither henchmen nor mercenaries, but admittedly our aims were basically sociological rather than aesthetic. As far as I could make out, we were Left-wing to a man, but I never knew of a Party member amongst us. And we knew, from viewing the monotony of Fascist and Communist propaganda, what a kiss of death such slanting meant to any-thing artistic. At the same time, as Mayerhold has said 'Art cannot be non-political.' Our aim was to make work an honour-able theme, and a worker, of whatever kind, an honourable figure, and, that, as a hidden threat to the *status quo* of that time, was subversive. Tallents was advanced and liberal, and understood all this very well, so we always had someone to answer the whispers in the corridors.

47

Anyway, Donald Taylor had to make a film for the Ministry of Ag & Fish. It was actually about intensive market gardening, but, as I said, Taylor really hankered after the big time, and decided to open the film with an acted sequence. I'm sure he never told Grierson about it. Obviously, when starting to think about the subject, before he got down to the exciting statistics of how many carrots you got to an acre, he remembered 'In Spring, a young man's fancy lightly turns to thoughts of love.' He had got hold of the most fashionable model of the time, Nina Keetch—who was equally famous for having been married to the man who taught the Prince of Wales to play the ukelele—who said she'd do the part for nothing; but he funked hiring an actor, so decided to choose me! One look at Nina, and I was game. (They told me long afterwards that I was good-looking when I was young. Thank God I didn't realize it.)

It was a beautiful spring morning when we set out in George Noble's old Bugatti for the country house that Donald Taylor had borrowed for the day. George drove like a fiend, but very expertly. So we arrived near our location just before lunch. With a quick wink at Nina and me, George swung into a swagger road-house. Donald, who had been brooding on the job ahead, woke up just in time to protest weakly 'Won't it be a bit expensive?' But Nina was out and gave him a ravishing smile, and he was lost.

We had a smashing lunch, real feature stuff—none of the usual bolted bread and cheese in the nearest pub. Finishing with double brandies, we were feeling no pain at all when we started to rehearse, and by now Nina and I rather fancied our parts. Donald's brain-child was about the most awful piece of corn imaginable. I had to chase Nina round a sort of phoney fountain hanging with flowers, and then, with extraordinary quick thinking, double back, catch her in front of the camera, and kiss her. Boy, did we make a meal of it! We had six takes, each a bit more athletic than the last, with George egging us on, and Donald still dreaming of his name in lights. We had to hold the end of each take, because the big idea was that it was to be a dissolve into someone spreading manure or something equally active and real. The hold for the dissolve was about the most active and real thing Donald ever shot.

Funnily enough, none of us seemed unduly nervous at the rushes. But by the end of the first take, one could almost see the clouds of wrath gathering over Grierson's head. The shot was a stinker, and the long end close-up positively revolting. I was cowering in my chair, sick with embarrassment. I had had no idea I could be so awful. I looked like a half-witted, sex-starved farm boy taking bites at a melon. (I also realized why film actors are so egocentric. Although Nina was exquisite, I never looked at her, but followed myself through each take, albeit with horror.)

By take three, Grierson was quivering, and as take four started, he barked 'Stop it!' We signalled to Pat, but he was so fascinated by the action that he didn't see us, so we all jumped up and started yelling 'Stop it', like a posse from the Purity League at a strip-show. Take five had got to its ghastly climax before Pat twigged.

Grierson glowered at us for about ten seconds. I think he was, for the first and only time in his life, speechless. Finally he said, quite mildly, 'Burn it', and left.

We did burn it. But first George and I cut out the best frames to show our pals in the pub.

I never acted again.

*   *   *   *   *

I was getting nowhere fast, and I was a bit apprehensive when Joe Golightly told me 'The Chief' wanted to see me. He always called Grierson 'The Chief', which we rather baulked at. There was a unit rumour that Grierson had saved him when he was just about to commit suicide over some cliffs, but none of us could really visualize Grierson in the role. He could have argued him out of it, perhaps.

I was apprehensive because a number of people had appeared and disappeared rather smartly during the last few months. There was a bloke called Clark—I wonder what happened to Clark?—he had all the qualities of a tycoon—and then J. N. G. Davidson, a charming and quite beautiful Irishman. George Noble brought about his downfall, too. They were sent off to get some lyrical shots of the countryside, for a travelogue, which demanded sunshine and lovely clouds. Somewhere on the way to their location, George acquired one of those little Swiss weather-house forecasters, where the man comes out if it's going to rain, and the woman if it's going to shine. They found a congenial hotel, and shared a bedroom. Between the beds George placed his Swiss gadget. Whatever the weather was like outside, they abided by their barometer. The fact that Grierson called on them on one of summer's hottest days, and found them asleep, led to the end of JNG, and a considerable cynicism on George's part about the mechanical efficiency of the Swiss. Grierson never blamed the cameraman. He was an employee—a skilled and helpful one, admittedly—but the responsibility for the shots, the set-ups, the mood and the discipline, was the director's. He never allowed a cameraman to go out on his own. Juniors like myself went out with old hands like George Noble, and I was in charge—and carried the can for everything except bad photography.

Grierson was looking at a letter when I went in to his office, and he started straight off, 'I want you to go to Ireland. Bob Flaherty wants a young man with a strong back.' I had hoped that some mention might have been made about mental capacity, but at least I wasn't being fired. Grierson went on, 'He's making a film on some rock in the west of Ireland. It'll mean roughing it.' I made the kind of expression I hoped meant 'That's all right with me, Boss—we seamen, you know.' Considering my acting in Donald Taylor's film, I'm sure it looked more like I was trying to hold back a fart. What I was thinking was 'Will I get any more dough?' Grierson read my mind. 'You'll get a quid a week more, and your keep, of course. It'll be a great experience for you—Bob's a great film-maker.'

I was excited and delighted, and lashed out on oilskins, sea-boots, long woollen underwear and lots of gloves. I really believed—and I think Grierson did too—that we would be on something like the Eddystone Lighthouse.

I was therefore extremely surprised when I saw my rock loom out of the haze of Galway Bay. It was a considerable island, about seven miles by three, dotted with cottages, and with a fair-sized village huddled round the pier at Kilronan. I was met by Pat Mullen, a tremendous man, rugged and extremely handsome, the uncrowned king of the island. He was Flaherty's general fixer, rounding up extras for the film, hiring the help and so on. He also had one of the most persuasive lines of blarney that I have ever met in a lifetime amongst bull-merchants. He heaved my battered suitcase into the jaunting car, and off we went. I still imagined we might be going to some hidden promontory with a gloomy ruin towering on the cliffs, but we only got as far as Daly's pub. The horse stopped instinctively, as Pat told me that all the Flaherty guests had a drop there for the journey. 'Ah, maybe we are going out to a rock—it could be tough, better have a stiffener', so I followed Pat into the dark little hole that was the centre of Kilronan's convivial life. I forgot that Irish measures were about double ours, so was ready for any journey by the time we climbed back into the car. The road was rocky, but passable, and meandered between enormous high dry-stone walls, that zigzagged everywhere. The height of the jaunting-car enabled me to realize that behind the walls the tiny fields were lush with spring grass, and some fine cattle grazed on it. From the sea, the maze of walls had blended into one grey mass, and given an appearance of desolation and barrenness. But although the people were poor, they weren't starving.

About a mile further on, I got my great surprise. We rounded a corner—and there, perched on a little mound by a lovely oval beach, was a typical Devon or Dorset holiday villa. If it had been called Mon Repos or Bide Awee you would have shuddered but made no comment. 'There, Mr Watt'—again pronounced to rhyme with fat—'is the headquarters of the fillum *Man of Aran*!' No tents clinging to rocky ledges, no prefabricated huts with their roofs held down by slabs of stone, no ruined castles with gloomy keeps, in fact no reason at all for me to spend all that money in the Army Disposal Stores. Just a rather ugly villa. It was a pretty fair anti-climax to my silly imaginings. (I found out afterwards it was built by a retired teacher from Birmingham.)

The film unit was having lunch when I was shown in. Later, I was told that Mrs Flaherty had described me as 'a little tipsy'. But as all Flaherty's guests who were met by Pat Mullen arrived in something of the same state, no other comment was made.

The luncheon party consisted of Bob Flaherty, who was, as always, a marvellous host, Mrs Flaherty, looking rather like one of the Daughters of the American Revolution, Bob's brother

David Flaherty, the editor John Goldman, one of Flaherty's several daughters, and John Taylor, who was assistant cameraman, and in charge of the laboratory, and whose contribution to *Man of Aran*, and many other fine films, has been shamefully underestimated. He was a quiet, shy young English boy, and my lifelong friendship with him was, for me, the best thing that came out of that long stint. Later on he married Pat Mullen's daughter Barbara, who became one of Britain's most popular television actresses.

After lunch I was shown my quarters. About fifty yards from the main house, a series of Irish cottages had been built, ostensibly as sets, but I never saw them used as such. They housed Goldman, Taylor and me in considerable luxury, and were also the cutting-rooms and projection theatre. We had a bedroom each, and a communal living-room, with a huge open fire. We even had a billiards table.

I settled down to the easiest six months I had had in five years. I never quite understood what I was there for. We had two grown men, with much stronger backs than I would ever have, just to heap the peat turf on the fires. When we went on location, what with donkey-carts, jaunting-cars, eager extras, and helpful hangers-on, I was lucky if I could carry a lens-case. My main job became helping John Taylor, who had fitted up and ran the laboratory. This was a *tour de force*. In a tin shed, stuck on the concrete slipway just above high-water level, John developed and printed—alone and largely by hand—the quarter of a million feet of film that Flaherty churned out. When one recalls that this was a cameraman's film, and is mainly memorable for its photography—some of the best of which was also shot by John—I've always thought that John Taylor deserved just about equal credit with Flaherty.

Because I didn't enjoy myself on *Man of Aran*, I find my memories of that time are rather blurred. Perhaps it is wrong to say I didn't enjoy myself. I was young and carefree enough to have a marvellous time, shooting and fishing, drinking vast amounts of free Guinness, and enjoying the adventures of the basking-shark hunts. But at the EMB, I had just begun to realize that I might have some ability to do something worthwhile, which, in the wee small hours of the night, I had begun to doubt. I had had the wonderful luck of having been caught on the brink of becoming just another drifter. But I needed, and enjoyed, discipline. And there was none of that on Aran.

Robert Flaherty was a mining engineer who had been sent up to northern Canada in the early twenties to look for iron-ore, when the Hudson Bay Railway was going to open up the country. He took a ciné-camera with him, and photographed the Eskimoes and their way of life when he came across them. He didn't find iron, but, bitten by the film bug, started to try and edit the material he had shot. Unfortunately, he did this while smoking a cigar, and the nitrate film of the time blew up in his face, and he spent six weeks in hospital. His whole film, negative and positive, was gone forever. Somehow he persuaded Revillon Frères, a French-Canadian fur company, to back him to go back to the north to film again, and out of this trip came *Nanook of the North*, one of the all-time classics. It got world-wide acclaim, and Flaherty became a film-maker. He went to the South Seas and made *Moana*. He tied up with Hollywood and tried again with a well-known producer called Murnau. But Flaherty was a loner, and difficult to work with. His films took an interminable time to make, and seldom showed a profit. I think he only had about half a dozen sponsors in his whole life.

He had come to England at Grierson's invitation, and had made a fine two-reeler called *Industrial Britain*. It was a study of the traditional tradesmen and skilled artisans of the North and Midlands, the glass-blowers, the makers of fine machinery, the people on whom Britain had built up her industrial supremacy. Flaherty's camera caressed their beautiful hands and worn faces in a way that has hardly ever been matched since. He was an utterly instinctive cameraman. You could see him loving his subject through his camera. But somehow they remained exquisite objects, and hardly ever living, sweating, smelling human beings. No-one in Flaherty's films, as far as I can remember, ever spat, or retched, or even seemed to want to copulate, lovely though they were.

Which was all the more remarkable because Flaherty was about as male a man as I've ever met. He was a magnificent drinker and giver of parties—in fact, one of Mrs Flaherty's principal job was to prevent Bob spending the money he got for a film on parties to celebrate the fact that he was going to make a film. Anyone who has been in on one of Bob's yarn-spinning sessions—which often went on all night—will never forget them. As so often happens, he couldn't put these down on paper, and the books he tried to write were flat and trite. In fact, he put little on paper. When I got to Aran, there was a page torn from a notebook stuck up on the notice-board which said '*Shots Wanted.* Seagulls, and shots of Maggie carrying seaweed.' That paper was still on the board when I left after many months, and it was the only semblance of a script I ever saw. Maybe somewhere there was an outline of the theme, but I doubt it.

I don't think Grierson and Flaherty got on. Perhaps that was why Grierson sent me out to Aran. Certainly their overweening personalities must have clashed. Bob was once heard to say, with drink taken, 'What's wrong with British Documentary is that it hasn't any balls.' And he had a point there. Although we were apparently physically intact, our films, up to that time at any rate, were a bit niminy-piminy, influenced no doubt by the social standards of the time. But we were just starting, we had no money, lousy equipment, and the dead-hand of Government sponsorship to contend with. Given Flaherty's scope of subject, his unlimited time, his—to us—colossal budgets, and the studio equipment he had at his disposal, I think several of us might have matched him. And our films would have had more balls than his ever had.

In all fairness and honesty, this must be qualified. We could never have matched the unique quality of Flaherty's films, which is very difficult to define. What fascinated him about the Eskimoes was the vividness and even gaiety of their life under the most appalling physical conditions. He set out to explore this, and his film career was one of continued exploration into how primitive people coped with their existence. Because of this fixation, he never really knew where his films were going, and his famous and interminable tests at the beginning of each picture were like questing searches up the tributaries of a river. Out of them came lyrical impressions, paintings if you like, that stay in the memory long after the other films of the period are forgotten.

What I enjoyed most in Aran was the constant stream of

visitors who poured over to see Flaherty. The Dublin intelligentsia were almost always with us, people like Oliver St John Gogarty and Liam O'Flaherty. And lots of friends from the States and Canada. Everyone knew the booze and the talking would be good if Bob was around. Of all those that came and went, the one I remember best was Captain Murray, a retired sea captain. He wasn't actually a visitor, but a new member of the unit. He had come to help us on the basking-shark sequence. Every year these huge harmless sharks—they look more like whales, and grow to about thirty feet long, and three to four tons weight—pass slowly up the west coast of Ireland. On calm warm days they drift just below the surface of the sea, with their great black dorsal fin cutting quietly but apparently menacingly through the water. They live only on plankton, and never harm anyone or anything on purpose. We used to go out in rowing boats and dig them with an oar to make them jump.

Flaherty discovered that, about a hundred years ago, the Aran islanders used to hunt the sharks in the currachs—their home-made canoes—to get oil from the livers to light their lamps. So he decided to have a shark-catching sequence. This was where Captain Murray came in. He was the last surviving skipper of the Dundee whaling fleet, who used to set off in tiny sailing schooners for the extreme north of Canada, on voyages of two or three *years*. He was a quiet dry little man, with a lilting east coast accent, and a fuzz of hair growing out from his nostrils, that I had to pull out when they got too long and tickly. It was when he got to know us juniors better, and we relaxed over our Guinness in front of the fire, that he started to tell us of his voyages. And they were hair-raising. They could only get the dockside scum to sign on for these trips, and many of them were more or less hijacked when they were too drunk to notice. They sailed in the early spring to get as far north as they could as the ice broke up. Each ship went her own way, and tried to find new and unfished waters. This meant penetrating into completely unknown areas, where even explorers had never been. They were, of course, right out of touch with the world, and there was just no hope if things went wrong. It was much more dangerous than the Pacific or the South Seas whaling. Captain Murray told us of riding out gales anchored to icebergs, of open boats capsizing, and men freezing to death, but it was his stories of the winters that really horrified us.

When the Scottish whalers sensed the winter coming on, they made for the land, and searched out an Eskimo settlement. They then anchored and allowed themselves to be frozen in. The Eskimo men brought their womenfolk aboard, and they were lined up for inspection. The Captain had his pick, then the mate, and so on down the line of seniority until there were no more women left. The payment was in axes, knives and booze. Then the whalers settled down in their self-made hell for the six months of Arctic winter, in complete darkness most of the time, and with the gales constantly howling through the rigging. They had nothing to do but fornicate, fight, and drink. Captain Murray, night after night, in a quiet soft voice, told us of death, madness, bravery and treachery. One of the very few I remember now was of an Eskimo who claimed a skipper had cheated him on the price of his woman, and accused him of it while the skipper was in his bunk. When the skipper told him to get out, the Eskimo ripped his guts open 'from bellybutton to crutch' with a blubber knife. The wounded skipper had the Eskimo seized and slung up to the yard-arm. He then took pot-shots at the swinging body with a pistol in his right hand, while holding his guts in with his left. They both died lingering and horrible deaths. These were not stories of the brutality and callousness of the seventeenth or eighteenth centuries. This was almost now. This simple little man, sitting there in his carpet slippers and with his glass of beer in his hand, had witnessed many of these things. As a young man, he had sometimes spent *two* winters cooped up in those hell-holes, watching the utter degeneracy of man, and the systematic corruption of a primitive people. His stories were endless, and I never took a note. If only it had been the age of the tape-recorder. This was history with the lid off, and I missed it. When I got back to London, I persuaded the girl who later became my wife to go up to Dundee and try and take down Captain Murray's life story. But he completely clammed up in front of a woman. I don't suppose he even told his wife. He died soon afterwards, and the true story of the Dundee whalers—which, despite the gruesome and bloody details, was one of epic endeavour and enormous physical courage—was lost forever.

After the basking-shark sequence was finished and Captain Murray had gone, I began to get more and more restive. It was partly the dreary job I had so often to do. This was in the lab with John Taylor. When the thousands of feet of film from Flaherty's indiscriminate shooting came in, we two youngsters often had to work day and night in the smelly cold uncomfortable tin shed. This was boring enough, but it wasn't helped by the fact that often we knew that the stuff we were working on was repetitive or irrelevant. Without a tight script, there is always over-shooting and waste on a film. This led me to my main discontent; I felt I was learning nothing. I daresay this could be said to be my own fault, my own mental laziness. Throughout my life so many people have said how lucky I was to work with Flaherty. But what was happening, I realized later, was that, sub-consciously, I was beginning to realize that I had been given a small instinctive talent for dramatic journalism. I was able to see and select the events in ordinary people's lives that made them exciting and moving, and dramatize this into a film document. Although this creative conceit was only a glimmer at that time, the interpretation of life on Aran that was taking place was worrying me. Because, as a piece of realism, to me the film was a phoney. Flaherty has been written of as the doyen of documentary. But what he was doing on Aran was not, again to me, documentary. It was a romanticized pictorial record of what may have been the island's way of life about a hundred years back. That was all right, but when I realized that it was going to be presented to the world as the truth of that present day, and when I saw that the real life of the islanders was just as exciting and dramatic in a different, but much more human way, I decided to get out.

What precipitated it was Flaherty's reaction to my only constructive suggestion to him about the film. I found out that on one of the nearby islands—there are actually three Aran Islands —there occurred once a year an interesting and, to me, exciting and pictorial event. All the cattle to be sold that year were herded down onto the only beach, and then pulled out one by one through the surf to a waiting steamer. The cattle sensed their danger, and went mad, so the scene became a sort of Irish rodeo. But there was also the underlying drama that the cattle represented to the islanders their total capital for that year, the proceeds of which bought the rising necessities in a changing world. A broken leg, a sudden panic in the water, and the annual ham, the oil for the lamps, the new boots for the children, would have to be gone without. And when the swell was high, there was constant danger to the men—none of whom could swim, of course—launching and relaunching their flimsy canoes, each with a battling bullock tied to the stern.

I thought it was a worthwhile idea to put forward. I was far too young and inexperienced to be hurt if Flaherty found the scene would not fit into his scheme of things. But his reason for turning it down shook me. He didn't want to show that the islands were serviced by a steamer! This was cheating. So I was not unhappy when it came my time to leave.

*   *   *   *   *

My return to Oxford Street made no impact at all. All I got was 'Hullo, how was Ireland? Christ, you've got fat! Look, pop over to Studio Film Labs and see if they've got the titles for the banana film ready. And make sure they've spelt my name right.' There had been some changes, though. Donald Taylor had married Marion Grierson, and gone off to form Strand Films. A new editor, McNaughton, had joined us. And we'd got sound. The cheapest that could be bought. The Americans had all the good sound systems tied up by patents, and they were therefore prohibitively expensive. We had to settle for a sort of pirated British system, Visatone, that had no 'squeezed track' to keep down background noise, so that there was a constant gravelly hiss whenever the sound-track functioned. We only used it for commentaries and sounds effects. I think we were all a little afraid of it. We realized that it had to be used creatively, but as yet didn't know how to do that. In fact, all it meant was more problems for people just beginning to understand their jobs.

As usual, there were various rumours running around the Unit, the two most interesting being that Grierson was going to get married, and that the Unit was under scrutiny from some Government Committee, which had the power to close us down as an unnecessary expense. The first rumour surprised us the most. In the Empire Marketing Board, legitimate sex was out. Grierson knew some of us were living in sin, and chose to ignore it, but we were specifically ordered not to marry. Grierson was said to believe that wives came between men and their creative impulses. It all sounds exaggerated and almost impossible nowadays, but when I did marry shortly after this, my wife was ordered away from a location, although she was working like hell for nothing. And now the autocratic old sod was weakening. We were delighted. He finally married a charming girl who helped to cut our negatives, Margaret Taylor, sister to John Taylor, my pal on Aran. Rather pathetically, Grierson pretended for almost a year that he wasn't married to Margaret, although we giggled happily with her about it.

The buzz about our possible closure didn't perturb us as much as one might have expected. Our existence had always been precarious, and our function so peculiar to the Government mentality of the time that we always seemed to be living in limbo. Whenever an economy campaign was suggested, our tiny grant of about £15,000 was the first that seemed to spring to mind for axing. On the principle of kicking the office cat when the profits fall, I suppose.

I was soon made assistant to Edgar Anstey, on a two-reeler (twenty minutes) called *Six-Thirty Collection*. This was one of a number of films we were being asked to make for the Post Office, who seemed to be becoming more and more aware of the value of indirect propaganda. It was to be an account of how the Post Office coped when, in late afternoon, an avalanche, a tidal wave of mail—the heaviest collection of letters of the day in the West End of London—poured into the Western District Sorting Office, next door to Marshall & Snelgrove's, and how, within a few hours, it was on its way to everywhere.

Edgar Anstey was a quiet, efficient, unflappable director, who went about his job in a straightforward way without any pretentious straining after effects, and none of George Noble's famous 'arty-farty'. We had an excellent cameraman called Onions, and I enjoyed working with them, and learnt more than on any other job I'd had. Everything was going fine, until, with about ten days shooting left to go, Anstey got another job!

It is very important, if one is going to give a true picture of our movement at that time, to explain that this wasn't just a matter of Anstey saying 'There's another couple of quid a week, up-you Jack, I'm off'. To start with, although all our

59

salaries were minimal, we were utterly loyal to Grierson and our idea. In these cynical days it would be looked upon as a joke, but we were, in a way, realistic disciples. Apart from that, there was, basically, nowhere else to go. We could have tried for the feature business, but this was overcrowded and insecure. Technicians were taken on picture by picture, which generally lasted about six weeks, were worked into the ground, and then flung out to hang around the breadline until another film came along. There was also the fact that 'the trade' despised us, and looked upon us as a lot of long-haired Left-wing intellectuals. We could even become trouble-makers. The fact that some of the best critics had begun to write about our efforts didn't influence them one bit. I don't believe they ever looked at our films. Certainly up to that time practically none had ever been shown in a commercial cinema. A few of the very large corporations, however, like Shell and Imperial Airways, had begun to realize that here was a medium to put across their overall aims and public image and were starting to flirt with the idea of commissioning films or even setting up units of their own. Grierson, knowing better than any of us how chancy was our existence, was very much alive to these moves. He was also a shrewd politician and operator, and knew the best way to keep his finger well into these pies was to place one of his own boys wherever there was a new opening. So, Anstey was suddenly whisked off *Six-Thirty Collection* and went to Shell.

I was told nothing of these manœuvres, and was merely informed that Anstey had gone, and that I was to finish the film. I was naturally delighted, and didn't feel nearly as frightened as I had been over my three original post-box shots. Everything had gone so smoothly, that I just carried on in Anstey's footsteps, leaning heavily on Onions the cameraman, who was wonderfully helpful, and didn't try and patronize me one bit. It would have been amusing to have been able to write a dramatic piece on the lines of the understudy taking over at the crucial moment after the prima donna had swallowed a wasp, but it wasn't like that at all. We just plodded along for the allotted ten days, packed up our gear, thanked the long-suffering sorters and postmen, and left. But it represented a tremendous lift in my career. As I said earlier, the first and greatest rule for succeeding in show business is 'Get the Breaks'.

Back at Oxford Street, I assembled all the material, eliminated the duplicate takes and obviously dud footage, and wondered what would happen next. Grierson ran the whole assembly by himself one day, and I got a message, via Golightly the grapevine, that he was pleased with what I'd shot. I accepted this with a good deal of smugness, but then I got one of Grierson's famous chits, telling me to edit the film! *I* couldn't edit. I could join film, I could cut out false starts and camera flashes, but I could not edit. It was plain daft, but I wasn't going to say so. I knew Grierson's sink-or-swim theory, and I knew if I had said I could not do it, I might very well never get another chance. (I can see now that Grierson's attitude was quite the wrong one, and could have led us to disaster with too much amateurism and lack of polish. What saved us was the arrival of Cavalcanti, a real professional.)

I joined all the material together in chronological order, and ran it. It was about an hour of unadulterated boredom. After all, once you post a letter in a pillar-box, there is little that can happen to it, except the process of collecting, sorting and delivering. They have been known to have been blown up by the IRA, or covered with swarms of bees, or even eaten by a plague of snails, but such scenes would hardly fit into a film financed by the Post Office to emphasize its modernity. The film I was looking at showed the processes perfectly, but about fifty times too often. I took out what I considered was every superfluous shot, and it was now only five times too long! I was in despair, and thinking of throwing in the towel and asking for help, when I was saved by the bell.

The Government Committee that was deciding our fate had decided to play fair, and let us at least plead our case. They would have a look at what we were doing. But being busy men, they could only spare us two hours. So a directive came round to all the directors and/or editors, that resumés of the work in hand should be prepared for the following week. My quota was eight minutes. The directive also emphasized how vital it was that these extracts should be entire in themselves, and give as clear a pattern as possible of what the picture was trying to say. My first reaction was, of course, that it just could not be done. Here was I, with an hour of film, every foot of which seemed essential to describe the continuity of action we had set out to explain, and I had despaired of cutting it down to twenty minutes without making it incomprehensible. But eight minutes! It was impossible. However, the executioners were on the way, and desperate measures were needed. I broke the whole film down again into a bin, and then selected the one best and most vital shot of each process, from post to collecting, through the various methods of sorting and franking, to the packing, addressing and shipping out to the trains and aeroplanes. I joined them together, trying to keep a continuity of movement in one direction, and—Jesus, I had a film! It moved and it made sense! Inadvertently, I had been taught the first rule of a good cutter—be ruthless. Cut out the deadwood, and use only that one essential shot that tells your story. And to hell with the director and the cameraman and the producer who are breathing down your neck, and screaming that they spent three days hanging upside down from a tree to get that scene. If it doesn't add to the story, junk it. Practically every film I've ever seen—including my own—has been too long. It's so hard to throw away the results of the dreadful endeavour that the making of films always is.

I never became much of an editor. I was always too clumsy and impatient. But the enforced discipline of that Committee showing taught me an awful lot that I never forgot. It taught me to shoot for cutting, and to look and look for the real essentials. This saves the dithering and waste of time and film that comes from indecision, and from lack of research in the preliminary and scripting period of a film. And shooting for cutting, directly from a tight script, is essential when making any film with a story.

The inspection committee duly arrived, after a chaotic last-minute rush from all of us to get the film excerpts ready. We listened to the solemn procession from Grierson's office to the theatre, and sneaked glimpses of the alien black suits and stiff collars through the cutting-room doors. We quizzed young Pat to see if he knew how the films had gone, but he had been so petrified of making a mistake that he'd kept his eyes glued on his machines.

Apparently, the pundits liked the films very well. They particularly enjoyed *Six-Thirty Collection*. As this was about as straightforward a piece of childish explanation as had ever been assembled, they understood it perfectly. They told Grierson he had obviously gathered around him a band of talented and creative young people, went happily back to Whitehall, and chopped us.

3

We were summoned together by Grierson and told we were
going to be moved over to the Post Office. Although it was a
matter of take it or leave it, we were depressed and fed-up. We
had done some films for the Post Office, and they were pretty
uninspiring. What we had been asked to do for it was describe
a certain process, and we had done this efficiently, but with
very little creative imagination. This was our fault, and not the
Post Office's. But now we pointed to these films and felt certain
that this would be what we would have to make from now on.
What we rank-and-filers did not realize was that we were being
taken over to the Post Office by Sir Stephen Tallents, that most
understanding of men, and that we would find, amongst the
faceless little squares we imagined were hidden away in the
bowels of the administration, some of the most easy-going
and sympathetic patrons an experimental unit could wish
for.

Using the modern word 'squares' makes me think how similar
we youngsters were to the much maligned kids of today. To start
with, we were equally scruffy. Our uniform was appalling
flannel trousers, usually much too baggy, a not too clean check
shirt, a stained pullover, and a dreadful tweed jacket, with
bulging, sagging pockets, and, more often than not, a tear
somewhere. We were completely improvident, spending what
money we had on booze or girls. We were very politically conscious, and were fiercely anti-Fascist and anti-Nazi. We
demonstrated constantly during the Spanish Civil War period,
but, to our shame, did nothing very constructive, except contribute large slices of our tiny salaries to the International
Brigade. (We were always politically suspect to the Establishment, and at one time a Special Branch man was introduced as
a learner-editor. He was so obvious to everyone, that we made
his life a hell by constantly talking of bombs, kidnapping, and

assassinations. So much so, that he soon chucked his hand in. He came back, however, to marry one of the secretaries, and used to drink with us in our local.) But we were tremendously hard workers, ignoring set hours, and happily dossing down on the cutting-room floor if the job called for it. That may seem to indicate that I think that modern youngsters are not hard working. I believe they are, just as much as we were, if they have something to be really interested in. The trouble for creative kids of today is that they must feel that everything has been done. Which leads to stunts and gimmicks, and a straining for effect that they know, inside themselves, is phoney.

There was no great upheaval in the move to the Post Office. But three very important things happened. We took over much better premises at 21 Soho Square, which stayed the head-quarters for documentary right until the end of the war; we acquired a small studio at Blackheath, and Cavalcanti joined us. This last was by far the most important. I will categorically state that British documentary films would not have advanced the way they did from then on without Cav's influence.

Alberto Cavalcanti was a Brazilian by birth, but had lived most of his life in Paris. There he became first an art director in cinema, and later, in the twenties, one of the leaders of a famous group of *avant-garde* and experimental film-makers. Several of the films he made at that time are recognized as classics of their kind, notably *Rien Que les Heures* and *En Rade*. But the way was hard for a young innovator, with no money and a mother to look after, especially when sound knocked everything sideways.

Much has been written of the primitive and bizarre methods used to record the first sound films, with the recordists shut up in sound-proof glass booths, and huge microphones hidden in bowls of flowers or disguised as Buddhas, towards which the artists had to project their voices. No-one had then conceived the idea of dubbing, that is, recording the sound separately, and marrying it to the lip movements. This meant that, so far, talking films had only been in the language of their source. America therefore stood to lose its enormous international market. One of the big US companies conceived the brilliant idea of making all their films in Paris, as the hub of Europe, and having multi-national casts. So you had the extraordinary situation of the

Americans shooting on a set during the day, and then French, German, Italian, Spanish and Portuguese artists and crews taking the same set over at night or at weekends. It was New Babelsburg with a vengeance and finally ended in chaos. But the money they paid was colossal and Cavalcanti fell for it. He signed a contract to make the Portuguese versions. He soon found he was just a hack. He had no say on the scripts or the sets, and, for speed and convenience, was supposed to shoot the scenes in the same way as the Americans had done them. He stuck it out for a while, and then suddenly just quit, contract or no, and came to London.

Cav was a tallish, good-looking man with large sad eyes behind his spectacles, but with a sudden flashing smile. He was usually the softest and kindest of men, with infinite patience and perseverance to see we got things right, but occasionally would go into a screaming Latin rage, which always made us laugh, as his charming fractured English got muddled up with Portuguese and French.

I've never known what arrangement he made with the GPO, although I'm certain he was never paid enough. It must have been difficult for Grierson when we technicians more and more turned to Cavalcanti with our problems, but he was honest and shrewd enough to realize how much more polished and professional our films were becoming under Cav.

Shortly after we became the GPO Film Unit, I was given my first film to make on my own, although some preliminary work had been done by Anstey. It was the description of the building of a huge new radio station at Droitwich, in Worcestershire. As it took more than a year to build, I went up every now and then to cover each phase, and did more menial jobs in between. I had, on the camera, a charming old chap called Bill Shenton. He had been, in the twenties, an ace feature-film cameraman, and had photographed most of the Betty Balfour pictures. But he had hit the bottle, and in the change over to sound, had got left behind. He had joined the small army of freelance cameramen who existed at that time, precariously wandering from newsreel to publicity film to documentary, taken on by the day, and always hoping that some bigwig would die, or foreign Royalty would arrive, or just that Derby Day would come round again. He would pop in on us regularly with a cheery

'Any work?', and when he got 'Sorry, Bill', he'd never moan or press, but just clatter down the stairs again, with a 'See you Thursday'.

When we got regular cameramen of our own, there was obviously less work for the freelancers. We lost touch with Bill, until we suddenly heard he'd been found dead. The coroner's verdict was starvation! Bill had spent his every penny on booze.

This tragedy was a great shock to all of us, but particularly to Grierson. He was training up youngsters, and he realized, if he'd only thought about it, what an asset Bill would have been, and how easily he could have found him a niche with us. He blamed himself bitterly, but it was really Bill's pride that killed him.

I was very lucky to have Bill with me on *BBC-Droitwich*. He was full of stories of feature film-making, something utterly unknown to me—I had never been inside a proper studio! He was such a kindly man that he was as eager as I was to make a success of my first solo effort and he worked his heart out. I found I had to let him slip away occasionally for a stiffener, but his photography was superb. We had, of course, no assistants, so together we humped the heavy camera gear all over the site and I even had to do a bit of electrical work again, with the usual results. I still remember falling down a flight of stairs while carrying a two-kilowatt lamp. As I lay at the bottom, certain that my left elbow was dislocated, I could see Bill's bright, watery eyes contemplating me anxiously from above. 'Is the bulb broken?' was all he said. And such was our dedication, that I didn't curse him.

Bill politely but adamantly refused to shoot from heights. The radio masts were then the highest in Britain, and I wanted a shot of the new building, as seen from the top. So, with a lot of leg-pulling from the steeplejacks, I did it myself, with no great pleasure. The shot turned out to be singularly unimpressive and lasts about a second and a half in the film.

I was always a very poor cameraman. I kept watching the action and forgetting the mechanics of the bloody thing. I remember once taking the second camera outside Buckingham Palace when we were filming the Royal Family going to open Parliament. At the rushes, my shot was so squint that the state coach was rushing smartly downhill. In the embarrassed silence that followed, Cavalcanti said, 'We will keep that shot for the revolution.'

I edited *BBC-Droitwich* into what I considered a reasonable shape, and took it, of course, to Cavalcanti. He saw it through and commented in his oblique way. Although a superb producer, who could spot every flaw—and what was much more important, know why it was a flaw and how to put it right—he was so gentle that he hated to hurt people's feelings, and so one had to evolve an interpretation of his remarks. He said (and I won't try to reproduce his accent) 'You have a nice little film, Harry. A little slow, perhaps, but building a house is a slow thing, is it not? But the end, it is so dull.' I was at once indignant, as I have always been when my creative children were criticized. At the same time I believe, absolutely, as a director, in the true function of the producer.

Ideally, the producer must be the catalyst for a director. He must stand outside the miseries and compromises of the day's shooting, and view the 'rushes' utterly objectively, thinking only of what the team set out to achieve and portray. No matter what excuses or alibis, he must tell the director whether he has succeeded or failed. If the producer is a technician, the director must eventually listen, despite the heartaches he has endured. I had only two such producers in my film life, Cavalcanti and Les Norman, with both of whom I had the most monumental rows. I would like to thank them for their patience and their help.

The end sequence that Cav found dull was a completely conventional piece of film presentation such as you still see daily— God help us!—in so-called documentaries on TV. To show what Cav did with it I'll try briefly to describe it. It was the starting up for the first time of the huge dynamos and motors that had been installed in the main control room. The camera pans slowly across the machines to reveal the massive switchboard. The man in charge then glances at the clock, nods to an assistant, and connects a shining copper knife-switch. Then another and another. Dials begin to register, needles to quiver. Inside their protective gratings, the motors begin to turn. And their low hum gradually rises to a screaming crescendo as they gain speed, and more switches are connected. The camera pans back from the board, across the motors to a window, beyond which the mast can be seen. The camera dissolves through to the foot of the mast, and then pans right up it to the top, set against beautiful clouds. There is a phrase or two of conventional music as the title 'The End' is superimposed. Fade out. What Cav did was to scrap the noise of the motors, and put a brilliant sound montage of topical radio programmes in its place. Today, this would seem easy and commonplace. But we had only two lousy channels and no money. So from the radio and records we pinched snippets of singers, comics, operas, orchestras, speakers, announcers, all the most recognizable of the day, and mixed and mixed them in and out of each other. We youngsters were brand-new to sound, and this was expertise we just did not have. It lifted my dull sequence into something imaginative and for those times utterly different, and I was delighted. But it had a number of peculiar consequences.

By some quirk of Wardour Street, the film got theatrical release. This was almost unprecedented. One of our main struggles was to get practical recognition from 'the trade', and our virtual failure to do so was one reason for the eventual split in the documentary movement. My first booking was to the London Pavilion, in Piccadilly Circus! No name in lights, but there, on the tatty times-of-showing board, was *BBC-Droitwich* sure enough. I savoured this on the Sunday, and decided to drop around on the Monday evening, and study the reactions of my public. When I got there, the bloody thing had gone! Where my opus had been, was some stinking Mickey Mouse! I rushed to the manager's office, and confronted him with 'What happened to the short?' Thinking his projectionist had missed it out of the programme, he started 'Oh, it's one of the latest of Disneys. Very funny. If you'd care to see it next . . .' I interrupted him with 'No, no, no. I mean the other short, the BBC one—I'm the director.' Scenting difficulties, his unctiousness disappeared, and he put on his lofty, dealing-with-problems act. 'I am afraid we had some trouble with our patrons last night over the end of that film. They didn't like all that peculiar music and—er—funny sounds at the end. I'm afraid they gave it the bird.' I started to question and bluster, but he wasn't going to waste any more time with some scruffy short-maker who thought he was God's gift to cinema because he had strung a few shots together. He ushered me out with 'If you care

69

to question my staff, they will confirm what I say.' I did question the ushers and usherettes, and they told me that a few drunks had whistled and shouted, but nothing very much. They were sweet and sympathetic, and one even said she liked my film. But it was only a short—a fill-up.

So my ewe-lamb, my first-born, was jerked!

Two more things happened to *BBC-Droitwich* which were pleasanter. In those early days of sound, the more intelligent critics were studying it to see what use it would be put to as an art-form. Caroline Lejeune was the radio film critic. In one of her programmes she ran two pieces of sound track. The first was from a Cagney war picture 'Stand-by, Number One Gun, load, fire—Crash, boom, clatter.' Lejeune said that it was obviously easy to guess the visuals from that sound. She then ran our end track, with its melange of sounds, and asked her listeners what visuals they could imagine from that? She then explained about counter-pointing sound—all new to cinema fans—and pointed out how sound could be used imaginatively, and hoped that it would continue to be so used more and more. This was a bit of a consolation to old Cav and me, but, as we were a couple of hams, I have a sneaking feeling we'd rather have had our work at the Pavilion.

The other happening was that I got my first review in a newspaper:

Manchester Guardian, 14 March 1935

'BBC DROITWICH'

Mr J. H. Watt's Striking Film

Four short feature films, two finding their material in the machine world and two returning to the natural beauties of mountain and sea, were trade shown at the Gaiety Theatre, Manchester, yesterday morning. Something was well done in each, but by far the most impressive film of the four was *BBC-Droitwich*, a study of the largest long-wave transmitting station in the world, made by J. H. Watt for John Grierson Films.

The story of its construction, from the moment that the BBC decided that a new transmitter was required until it was built, is presented briefly, faithfully, and in an imaginative way which lifts the film clean off the solid earth of documentation into the finer atmosphere of art.

The photography has a beautiful meditative quality, and the scenes have been so admirably put together that the movement and logic of a work in progress are made manifest. Excitement is even generated by the testing of the transmitter and the climax of broadcasting. All the parts of the technique, for which there is some more or less established standard, are faultless. Where *BBC-Droitwich* must startle most filmgoers is in its use of sound. Speech, music, and sounds of work are all part of the film rather than accompaniment, the voice of the testing engineer is used with dramatic effect in one episode, and at the close wireless music and news form the basis for a fine piece of impressionist cutting. . . .

Inevitably, they got my initials wrong. This, of course, infuriated me, and from that moment all my credits were Harry Watt, which, in show business, was easy to remember. It also pleased my mother, living with her memories.

I have been involved in newspaper publicity all over the world. Films and film-makers are news, and giving interviews and getting publicity is part of the business. I can categorically state that not one story I have given or been associated with, be it in Britain, Bolivia or Burma, has been accurately reported. Names wrong, dates wrong, credits wrong, the lot. Ernest Betts, a high-powered film critic of the *Daily Express*, was famous for this, and we once printed a notice and stuck it over his desk 'For Shirley Temple read Lon Chaney, for Clark Gable read Jean Harlow . . .' and so on. He didn't think it was funny.

*　　*　　*　　*　　*

Now that we had new and better premises, a studio (even if it was only about the size of a church hall), reasonable cutting-rooms and a decent theatre, a number of new recruits turned up, such as Jack Holmes, Stewart McAllister, and Elton's young brother, Ralph. The most exciting arrival was Humphrey Jennings, who was eventually to become one of the all-time greats in documentary. I only worked closely with him twice, but just to have him about was a delight, as he radiated enthusiasm and energy, and his very presence around the place seemed to engender enthusiasm. He was a tall, skinny, grinning individual, with no chin to speak of, and an inability to pronounce his R's. He had come more or less straight from Cambridge with a First, was a considerable painter, yet was deceptively tough, and broke all my theories about getting on with the workers, as everyone adored him. After a slow start he became, as Lindsay Anderson says, 'the only real poet the British cinema produced'. He was tragically killed in 1950 while making a film in Greece, and his work, particularly his war films like *Listen to Britain* and *Fires Were Started* have rightly become a sort of cult with serious students of cinema.

We were also invaded by an alien brigade—four permanent Post Office civil servants. With the increased staff and premises, expensive equipment and so on, the Post Office decided that we would have to be administered, and our haphazard method of budgeting organized. So four brave men from Mount Pleasant, the GPO headquarters, moved in. I never knew whether they volunteered or were just drafted, but, whatever it was, they must have had a shock. One can, perhaps, imagine them sitting at the same desk for twenty years, adding up and initialling accounts, or having formal little chats. 'Do you mind, Mr Simpson, if I have another look at your file, L.S.872/76?—I believe there is a discrepancy in the Lowestoft figures for June.' 'Of course, Mr Rayner, just sign for it here, will you?'

They were thrown head first from that ordered existence into our madhouse. In our outer office, through which most of our traffic passed, including the whirlwind that was Grierson, they were given four desks identical to the ones they had occupied so long at Mount Pleasant, but it was the only similarity that could have occurred to them.

All would be going along nice and quietly when the door would burst open and a dishevelled and apparently hysterical youth would rush up to one of the desks. 'Gimme thirty quid float, will you, Joe? I've got to catch the 4.05 to Birmingham—for Christ sake, Chick, get a taxi—I dunno what film it is, Elton wants a shot of some bloody factory they're blowing up, ask him—no I'm not insured.' Yell from outside door 'Taxi's waiting.' Yell back 'OK, tell him to hang on.' Back to bemused civil servant. 'Oh, and Joe, get 5,000 feet plus-x film on the train

72

tonight, will you? Parcels office—how the hell would I know who pays for it, that's your job, isn't it? 'Bye and thanks.'

I must record that those four stalwarts coped magnificently. They became integral members of the Unit, as enthusiastic as any of us about our aims and our productions. They straightened out our slapdash accounts for us, let us have subs when we were broke, acted as extras in our films, drank with us, and even telephoned frantic girl-friends when we'd been whisked off somewhere.

In fact, all our fears and suspicions about the Post Office as employers were groundless. In an extraordinarily easy-going, broadminded way, they became ideal sponsors for the 'most experimental film unit in the world outside Russia'. As long as we stayed vaguely within their framework and overall budget, Grierson persuaded them to let us have our heads. And we soon discovered the possibilities were endless.

When we joined them full time, we were bemused to discover that they were the largest employers of labour in the country, with fleets of vans and lorries, trains, ships, aeroplanes, and even their own underground railway. So we made a general film which ended up just spouting statistics, and was as dull as ditchwater. Then we saw our stupid mistake. The story of the Post Office was one letter, one telegram, one telephone call, one postman's round, one train or one ship. There was as much drama and humanity involved in these as in any fictional imaginings.

No great ripple seemed to have been created by our minor success with *BBC-Droitwich*. I merely started getting lent out again. We were getting known internationally, and when visiting film people wanted advice and help, they came to Grierson. And I was the one he fobbed them off with. An enchanting little American turned up, who travelled the world constantly with an enormous camera and a long-suffering wife, and made a ten-minute travelogue called 'The Magic Carpet of Movietone' *every week*! He wanted a strong helper, so there I was again. It was an exhausting but rewarding experience. He tore around London from dawn to dusk, his Mitchell camera and tripod on his shoulder, while I staggered after him with the batteries and the spare magazines. He was a superb technician, and with that instinctive camera eye that Flaherty had. But he knew why certain set-ups were right, and told their story in one shot, and he explained this to me while I was getting my breath back. He let me look through his camera, demonstrated why a yard one way or the other was wrong, and taught me more in the fortnight I was with him than I could have learnt in a year of my own trial and error. This business of the camera eye is a strange one. It seems to be a built-in thing. With experience, one becomes pretty good at camera set-ups, but certain people can walk into a dull suburban square, take a quick look round, and say 'That window there.' And when you get to it, the square is suddenly lovely, the proportions are perfect, and you've got a picture. It doesn't appear to be anything to do with sensitivity. I know two cameramen who, if you met them at a party, you would consider as louts. But they will produce the most superb pictures, with framing and lighting worthy of any painter.

My next loan was to the March of Time series. This was an extraordinary piece of film journalism that had hit the screens of America—and later the English-speaking world—with a tremendous bang. It was an offshoot of *Time Magazine*, itself a sensational new departure in reporting, which had created its own type of journalese, with outrageous inverted grammar, studded with unusual adjectives. No-one was just a crooked lawyer. He was 'pipe-smoking, bandy-legged, father of ten, ambulance-chaser John Smith, aged 43'. It is a style that is parodied to this day, but it made a great impact at the time. The magazine was so successful that they launched into films, and produced a once-monthly twenty-minute report on current affairs. Its impact was enormous, with a machine-gun commentary, poured out in Timese by a doomwatch voice, whose intonations became a sort of folk-joke. They decided they wanted to include more European and particularly British items, so opened an office in London. It was headed by Dick de Rochemont, a large, pleasant easy-going individual, brother of the overall producer in the States. This time I was not to be just a strong back, but a director! They had tried an item with a cameraman-director and it had failed. It is surprising how seldom a cameraman, however talented, makes a good director.

I began to enjoy myself immediately. We had lots of money to play with, so life in films became for me for the first time a little like what outside people imagined it to be, with hire cars, decent hotels, and even regular meals. The production methods were somewhat peculiar. Having found, or been given a subject, you wrote the commentary only in your version of Timese. You soon found this was just a trick, and easy to copy. It was also, as I said, easy to parody, and sometimes when I put in my piece, I wondered if the Yanks would think I was taking the micky, but they seemed quite happy. You then went out and shot to illustrate the commentary, word for word. I mean this literally, because the March of Time cutting was so frenetic that you had to produce about half a dozen shots to cover each short sentence. All the shots had to be static, except perhaps to follow something like an aeroplane taking off. The result was that you shot dozens of snippets around every scene, largely irrelevant, because all they were wanted for was to carry words. Then— and this shook me at first—the whole lot, commentary and film, was sent to the States for editing! There, the big boys really got to work. I did several items for them, and not one word of mine ever returned from New York. They had to use the film, of course, but they had so changed it around and re-emphasized it, that it was hardly recognizable. Not that they didn't do a marvellous job. They made our pedestrian efforts vital and vibrant, if, at times, a trifle inaccurate.

The two items I made that were most fun were on football pools and tithes. 'The Pools' had just started up, and were under considerable attack from many sides, the anti-gamblers and the vociferous do-gooders saying that here was just another temptation for the working man to starve his children. There was a fair chance that the Government might clamp down on the whole idea, so the pools promoters refused to cooperate with us in any way. Thus it became an exciting foot-in-the-door journalistic job. We hung around the main offices with hand-held cameras and long focus lenses, and waylaid personalities wherever we could. I remember being somewhat surprised in Edinburgh, when waiting by the enormous Rolls-Royce belonging to a leading promoter called MacLauchlan, to find a very Semitic gentleman indeed climb into it. He had an excellent Scots accent, however, when he told us to bugger off!

We got coupons being made out, being posted, arriving by the lorry load, new ones being sent out, shots of winners with their cheques, interviews with those for and those against, in fact everything but the mystery of what happened to the millions of coupons once they were delivered. And it looked as though we were stuck on this when I had a brainwave that endeared me to my boss. I suddenly remembered that a pal of mine at the GPO had had to make an instructional film for the Savings Bank on rhythmic sorting. Just as with the pools, millions of slips poured into the Savings Bank headquarters from post offices all over the country. These had to be sorted by girls, and some time and motion study expert had invented a rhythmic two-handed movement to speed it up. The film was a straightforward demonstration of how it saved muddle and strain, whilst being more efficient. Whether this was true or not didn't worry me. What I realized was that here were shots of hundreds of girls sorting slips of paper, and, by judiciously keeping them in long-shot, they could be football coupons. We paid the GPO a high price for the scenes, which pleased it, shipped them off to the States, and got a congratulatory telegram. They duly appeared in the March of Time as the first shots ever made inside a pools sorting office, and, strangest of all, nobody seemed to twig. We never had a cheep from the Post Office, the pools people, or even the girls.

We made the tithes item because it was causing a lot of controversy at that moment, and because it allowed us to show rural England to America in a dramatized way. In fact, this episode was the first British effort to get a full release on the American circuit. What was happening was that farmers, who from time immemorial had paid a tithe or tenth of their crop to the Church, now found it an onerous extra taxation, and were refusing to pay. The Church authorities, with their well-known Christian charity, started forced sales of the farmers' goods. When these were blocked or boycotted, the authorities actually started Flying Squad-type raids on farms, where, after a gabble of legal jargon, a tame auctioneer proceeded to sell off certain animals or goods on the spot. The farmers counteracted this by keeping *their* Flying Squads in the fields, in the shape of youths on motorbikes, so that when the Church convoy was spotted, the alarm went out, everyone dropped everything, rushed to the threatened farm, and then bid a penny for a stallion, or thruppence for a stack of hay. One or two intrepid dealers, who tried to bid properly, generally landed up in the manure heap. Good exciting stuff, right up my street. The Church, of course, refused to cooperate with us. So I conned confiding vicars into allowing me to show them preaching to seven old ladies and a deaf verger, and discussed with them the uses of their twenty-roomed vicarages. Then I reconstructed the whole of a raid on a farm, the Church militants approaching, the alarm going up, the rush from the harvest, the attempted sale and so on. It was the first time I'd tried this sort of thing and, come to think of it, I suppose it was the first time a dramatic reconstruction of a contemporary event had been done in British documentary, if the March of Time could be ranked as such.

I made one bad mistake. I employed an actor to play the part of the rogue dealer who tried to bid and got done by the farmers. He was some bit player I found in Charing Cross Road, and he was bloody awful. I was far too inexperienced to control him, and he hammed it up dreadfully. Luckily, the Americans knew nothing of English country types, and accepted it. But it taught me a salutary lesson. I never used another professional actor in any of my own films until I went into features nearly ten years later.

After a few months, I was beginning, inside myself, to get restive at March of Time. Once you learnt the trick of it everything was reduced to a sameness. (I imagine this was why the series eventually died.) Also, my efforts being returned from New York completely regurgitated was pretty frustrating. At the same time, it was eight quid a week, I'd been recently married, and they were nice people to work for. I was in a bit of a dither, when an extraordinary thing happened. It was announced in the trade press that Edgar Anstey had been appointed permanent director to the European March of Time! Immediately, of course, no matter what my inmost doubts had been, I was indignant. My bosses had often praised my work, and they had been particularly delighted when the tithes item had made the American circuit. So I went straight to de Rochemont and asked him why he hadn't at least offered me the job. He was obviously surprised, and said 'Didn't you know, Harry? We're very happy with your work, and asked Grierson if we could approach you to stay on permanently.' He tossed the copy of a letter across to me. It confirmed what he had said. I asked 'What did he answer?' De Rochemont told me that

Grierson had rung up, and said that I was his man, and to lay off. As Anstey had finished at Shell, they approached him.

I was furious. I felt like a chattel, so went straight to Grierson and asked him why he hadn't told me that the March of Time had wanted to sign me up. Then happened a moment that I have talked about very little, but thought about often. Grierson lied to me. He just said 'They didn't ask for you.' I had seen their letter, and I knew he was lying. And I said nothing.

What one must try to realize is that Grierson was our guru, our 'Chief', our little god, the man who had given us an aim and an ideal, who battled for us and protected us, and at whose feet we sat. We were adult enough to laugh at his foibles and play-acting, to joke about his verbosity and Calvinism, but, basically, we adored him and could not humiliate him. All this, I suppose, must have come to me in that flash, and a sorrow, because I waited for him to say something more, some little compromise, and he didn't, but just stared at me with those wonderful eyes. I was angry too, because he should have trusted me enough to have known that he had only to say to me 'I want you back' and I would have been happily there, humping cameras at four quid a week. I compromised in my mind by saying to myself that because he wanted me and maybe needed me, I should feel flattered. But it was never quite the same again.

Perhaps because of that episode, I seem to have a blank in my memory about what I did on my return from the March of Time. I imagine I just helped people out in various ways. We were still basically a communal body, and there was no false pride about working for each other. At the same time, because we split up into tiny units and went off to shoot all around the country, we didn't know much about each other's films until they were finished. We'd meet in the pub at weekends, say 'How's the picture going?', hear the inevitable stream of woes that every director or cameraman always seems to pour forth, and wait impatiently to tell our own miseries. One little point comes to my mind that still astonishes film people when they hear about it. Despite all this camaraderie, we always called each other by our surnames. It was Grierson's influence of course, but even now, when we old-timers have a reunion, it's 'Hullo, Anstey', 'Hullo, Elton', as though we had all been in

The Remove together. I never called Grierson John or Jack in my life, and was slightly shocked when, at the age of seventy, he called me Harry.

*   *   *   *   *

I was suddenly asked to report to the front office, where I found Wright and Grierson. I was still, of course, very much a junior. They told me that they had decided to make a film about a special mail train that ran nightly from London to Scotland, and that they wanted me to direct it. I was delighted and agreed at once, although, in point of fact, from the way we worked, it was an order. They told me something about the subject and showed me a rough outline that had been prepared. I was to go out and write a full script.

None of us were to know for many years that, from that short informal meeting, was to evolve one of the most famous documentary films ever made—*Night Mail*. It has been written up in every anthology of film history, is required study in the film schools of the world, was voted one of the ten best pictures ever made, and so on. But to us, at the time, it was just a routine Post Office job, and rang no loud bells when we had finished it.

I got in touch with the London, Midland and Scottish Railway and discovered, to my astonishment, that they had a film director. I arranged to meet him, and he turned out to be the only film director I've ever known who wore a bowler hat. He was happily making instructional films for the railway, on how to drive a spike into a sleeper and things like that, and I'm sure he must have cursed the day Watt appeared on his horizon. As the Post Office were major users of his railway, he'd been told to give me every assistance. I drove him mad.

The scripting research was reasonably straightforward. The train left Euston for Scotland every night of the year except Christmas Day, with a complete Post Office personnel, apart from the train crew. There were thirty or forty sorters, and a special gang for dropping and receiving mail *en route*. This was the unique feature of the journey. As the letters were sorted, they were bagged and carried to a man in the centre of the train. There the mailbag was carefully strapped into a heavy leather pouch, and this, in turn, was hung on the end of a long, hinged, metal arm by a slip-catch. At a set moment, the arm was swung out of the open door of the van, so that the mailbag hung suspended about three feet out from the side of the train. At regular points of the journey, usually rather remote, for safety's sake, a net had been set up by other Post Office personnel. As the train rushed by, the pouch hit the net, the catch slipped, and the bag was caught. At the same time, a bag, hung from a sort of gibbet by the people on the ground, was caught in a net let out from the train, and was catapulted into the van with an enormous bang.

All this took place while the train was thundering through the night at seventy miles an hour, and needed split-second timing. If the bag for delivery was swung out too soon, it would have been smashed off by a bridge or a tunnel, or could even have decapitated some unfortunate late traveller loitering on a platform. As it was often foggy or misty in winter, and there were no obvious visual aids, the timing of this operation had to be done solely by sound. So skilled were the workers of this operation, that they could tell exactly where they were by the beat of the wheels.

The only stop of the night was for thirteen minutes at Crewe, around midnight, where great quantities of mail were exchanged, and the London sorters swapped over with a new team. Then the train climbed up Beattock in the dawn, and thundered down into the heart of Scotland in time for the morning deliveries.

Having written a full treatment, I prepared to go into production. Our scripts were never as tight or detailed as feature films had to be. As our units were so small and cheap, we had no need to maintain a strict schedule, and with facilities often being delayed through red tape or the inexperience of sponsors, we found ourselves having to write up sequences as we found them. But even if it was only scribbled on the back of an envelope, I always tried to have a shooting script.

Wright was to be the producer, with Grierson, of course, in overall command, and Cavalcanti, on the sidelines, advising. The budget was, I think, £2,000—it may have been less. My whole unit consisted of Pat Jackson, now a first-class assistant, and either Jonah Jones or Chick Fowle, two marvellous Cockney kids, still in their teens, who had been trained up from

80

messenger boys to become superb cameramen. It is an interesting sidelight to Grierson's method of teaching to recall that he insisted that they should go regularly to the National Gallery, to study the lighting of the masters.

An unexpected recruit joined us at the last moment. It was W H Auden, the poet. With our growing prestige and publicity, a number of the intellectuals of the time began to want to know more about this new art-form, and Grierson had quite rightly told Auden that he'd better start by working on a production. I remember him as a tallish, clumsy-looking creature, even worse dressed than we were, with red knobby wrists and hands sticking out of a jacket that appeared much too small for him. Because of his shock of uncombed blond hair and rather blank expression I once described him as looking like a half-witted Swedish deck-hand—with a posh Oxford accent. He was unlucky, perhaps, to come to me at that moment. I had at last found myself, if that is not too corny a phrase. I was tremendously excited by my subject, and mad keen to make a success of it. I now knew that my life's work was to become a film director, and I was determined to be a good one. As a result, of course, I became harder, more ruthless and egocentric, and the people around me suffered accordingly. When I was writing this, I happened to ask Jonah Jones what I was like to work with in those days, expecting, as one's conceit always does, to be told that I was energetic but stimulating, or something like that. Jonah, always honest, said 'You were a proper rough 'un.' So poor Auden copped it. To me, at that moment, he was only somebody to run along the railway line with a spare magazine, and if he turned up late—as he was inclined to do— he got the hell bawled out of him. He was to prove how wrong my estimation of him was, and leave me with a lifetime's awe of his talent.

We started production with desultory connecting shots of trains passing in progressively darkening evening into night. This is helped by filters, of course, but is much improved by late evening light. There is always one marvellous shot to be stolen in the last moment of day before it is too late to get an exposure. I seem to remember so many hours spent waiting and waiting, praying that the clouds would stay right, for that ten seconds of magic. We used any express trains, of course, provided they had a class-six engine. The indefatigable train-spotters were hell in railway films. They could spot the wrong engine in the longest shot, and immediately pronounce the film a phoney.

We then decided to do the mail dropping and catching sequence, the core of the centre part of the film. We found it extremely difficult to do. Being, in a sense, still amateurs, we never considered the idea of faking it, but tried to work out how to film it in reality. Our equipment and facilities were still poor. I know there is nothing more boring than some old boy adumbrating about his working youth, when things were tough and men were men, but nowadays, as practically everyone understands cameras or tape-recorders, I am going to take a chance and try and explain, as simply as possible, how and with what we worked. I am tempted to do this by what happened to me recently on a filmed interview. A soundman stuck a microphone under my tie and a tiny transmitter in my pocket and said 'Go where you like, it's a radio mike.' The cameraman hand-held his 16mm camera like a rifle, zoom-lensed around with me wherever I went, and, in pouring rain and lousy light, we got perfect colour and sound. On *Night Mail* it was a little more difficult.

We were now using, on all location stuff, Newman-Sinclair cameras. These were so-called portable cameras, produced by an old established British firm in Whitehall. They were an aluminium rectangular box, worked by clockwork, with 200-foot magazines. We always worked with 35mm film, by the way, and 200 feet gave you only about two minutes' shooting time. These cameras were heavy and this plus their shape made them awkward to hold steady in the hand, so about 90 per cent of our shots were made from a tripod. There was no lens turret, so each lens had to be removed, packed away, and replaced from the lens box when a change was needed. This, of course, made fast reportage shooting almost impossible. The main snag of these cameras, which I may say were very reliable, was that the finder on the side, through which the director viewed his set-up, and watched and rehearsed the action before deciding on the final shot, showed the pictures upside-down! This took a hell of a lot of getting used to, and led to new boys getting permanent cricks in their necks, trying to see it right way up.

Our sound was housed in a large pantechnicon, painted the

lovely Post-Office red, and therefore could not be used in very inaccessible places. As it was always in demand for the various films in production, a director had to concentrate his sounds sequences into as short a period as possible, and shot most of his film silent. The microphones were clumsy, non-directional affairs, plagued by wind and extraneous noises. We had no generators, and if a mains electrical supply was not available, we relied on photoflood lamps supplied from wet batteries, which were heavy, clumsy, and, of course, always ran out at the crucial moment.

So we started to shoot the mail dropping sequence. We travelled in the van from London to Crewe for several nights, and got nowhere fast. Our lights weren't strong enough to balance the photography with the natural light outside. We ended up getting lots of travelling cut-ins, and staged the close-ups in a siding, as we should have done at the beginning. I had evolved the old idea of having a trainee under instruction to show the public how the mail exchange worked. We just used the regular crew, and they were stiff and self-conscious, although his nervousness made the trainee seem very real. People have often asked me how I found my 'actors' in my dramatized documentaries. I'm afraid it is a sad comment on the acting profession: you look for the extroverts, the bullshit merchants, the boring life-and-soul-of-the-party boys. They are the natural hams, but if you then wheedle and bully them down to some sort of naturalness, they're actors. I was only just realizing this theory during *Night Mail*, and some of the acted scenes still make me shudder a bit.

As I said, we got most of the mail-dropping sequence by a mixture of fake and reality, but we still lacked the final shot of the pouches being caught in the net at speed. This took place three feet out from the side of the train, so we couldn't rig up a fixed camera outside the train, as that would have been smashed off in no time. So Chick Fowle volunteered to hang out of a window, just behind the catching net, with a hand-held camera. It was bloody dangerous. Every now and then the net burst, and that would have been the end of Chick. As it was, his head would miss the picking-up gibbet by a few inches. The decision and responsibility was mine, and quiet, unemotional Chick was keen to try, so, in the tradition of all film directors, who to get their picture right will risk anybody's life—including their own, mind you—I agreed.

Just before the first pick-up and drop place after London, while there was enough light to get an exposure, Chick struggled half-out of a window about ten feet behind the apparatus. Pat and I hung on to his legs and prayed. All we could see was Chick's tensed bottom. The run up to the change-over position was endless. The train seemed to be going faster and faster, and I could see that ugly great black bag hanging on its sinister arm, and rushing inexorably at Chick's head. There was a sudden, frightening crash, as the pouch landed in the van ahead of us, and a faint 'OK' from Chick. We hauled him in, his eyes streaming with water from the rush of wind. We sat down and looked at each other for a long moment. Now it was over I think we all realized what a foolhardy thing it was to have done. Then Chick said 'I'm afraid it was a bit shaky' and we all began talking at once.

Our tiny unit worked away through that long summer, with three main highspots. We covered, with lights, the thirteen minutes of hectic activity during the stop at Crewe. How we managed to do it, I still don't quite know. I think we got one extra helper, but we were never more than four. During the day we put up the scaffolding, mounted and connected the lights, rehearsed the tracking shots, placated the station staff, made sure the people we needed for continuity were called for daily, and waited for 11.45 pm. Then we shot like mad for those precious minutes. No-one dare hold up the mail train, so off it went, and our platform was left silent and dark. But we weren't finished. We had to unload the cameras, clear away the cables, and generally tidy up. For young Pat Jackson the night had just begun, and I have quoted this example to cynical trade unionists to show what dedication really was. The up mail train for London came in at 12.30 am. With our exposed film now in tins, Pat hopped aboard, and dossed down on the mailbags. From Euston, he taxied to the laboratories, and slept in their waiting-room until the film had been developed and printed. Then he caught another mail train back to Crewe, and by mid-day we could run our rushes at the local cinema and start preparing for the next night's filming. Dirty exploitation, my comrade friends called it.

84

As a lifelong Socialist, and an early trade unionist, I always seem to have been at cross-purposes with fellow believers. Perhaps I should have had a union of my own. When the association of ciné-technicians got organized in the thirties, after an earlier abortive attempt, I, of course, said I would join. Grierson called me in, and tried to forbid it. I was astonished. I actually knew nothing of his politics, but from his writings and speeches I had assumed he was left-wing. His argument was that I was on the way to becoming a director, and, if I joined the union, I was classifying myself as a technician, or lower echelon in the hierarchy of films. If this was his real reason, it was pretty muddled thinking. I suspect he felt he had enough troubles without his juniors getting organized. I listened to him and joined the union. After the war, as a successful features director, often responsible for a quarter of a million pounds, I was elected to the union executive from Ealing Studios. It was the time of the first Labour Government, and the Chancellor of the Exchequer, Sir Stafford Cripps, was making the appeal that has rung down the corridors of power to this day: 'We must export or die.' There was full employment in the film industry, as the Rank and Korda empires were at their zenith, and conditions for the workers were good. Though it is not generally realized, films are perhaps the easiest and most profitable of exports. It may take half a dozen large ships to carry enough Jaguars to America to make a million dollars profit. Ten tins of duplicate negative film, in a box measuring four feet by two feet, and weighing perhaps forty pounds, can easily earn the same amount. I therefore took up Stafford Cripps's cry, and said we should work like hell for Britain, while making sure the workers, at all times, got their rightful return. To my astonishment and fury, I was called 'a lickspittle of the capitalists', a 'bosses' man', and worse. What particularly infuriated me, and I swear this is not snobbism, was that the people who called me the names were microphone assistants and the like, whose total responsibility in life was to see that their tiny piece of equipment was connected up properly. The tragedy was that Roy Boulting and I just finally said 'Up you' and left the committee. We should have hung on and tried to do some good.

We worked at Crewe Station for about a week, and were left with one ambitious tracking shot that was causing us all sorts of trouble. No matter what we did, we got reflections of our lights in certain windows. The long-suffering stationmaster spread all the tarpaulins he could find over the roof, to no avail. After a rehearsal, while we stood moaning and cursing, a platelayer, who had stood by watching our antics in considerable bewilderment, said 'What's trouble then?' I said 'It's that bloody glass —it's giving us reflections in the lens.' He lifted his enormous hammer and said 'This one?' as it crashed in fragments. I was quick enough to say 'That one too' before he ambled off. The stationmaster was shocked by the careless manner in which we handled our tripod.

Despite the chaos we were constantly creating throughout their whole system, the railway company's cooperation with us was tremendous. They laid on a replica mail train in Broad Street Station, London, for a night, to do the details and sound sequences to match into our Crewe stuff. We worked for fourteen hours non stop, and I can't recall much through the fuzz of fatigue. The wheeltapper, though, will always be remembered, as he became a gag in the unit. We started shooting at five in the afternoon, and a little chap in blue dungarees came up to me with 'You wanted me, guv?' I said 'Oh yes, thanks. Just hang on, will you? We'll get to you soon' and promptly forgot all about him. At about eight o'clock next morning, with dawn well risen, and all of us dead with weariness, the wheeltapper pops up, cheery as you like with 'OK, guv?' The chorus of 'Oh Jesus', 'Bugger it', 'Who the bloody hell —?' echoed round the grisly walls of the station. Somebody unpacked a camera, somebody switched on a light, and we immortalized him. From then on, a 'wheeltapper' became a shot that had been forgotten.

We decided that the interior of the sorting van would have to be done in our studio. So, while that was being prepared, I went north with Pat Jackson and Jonah Jones. We had one of the days of our lives, as we were given an engine all to ourselves to go up and down the famous Beattock climb into Scotland. We were still three youngsters and the fun and excitement of having our own engine was tremendous. We went up and down all day, the only serious moment being when Pat was nearly killed again. His enthusiasm and endless energy had led him to about four hairbreadth escapes already. We were trying to get a shot inside the engine cab, which turned out to be unexpectedly dark. So Pat climbed up onto the coal with a reflector. (Reflectors were large rectangles of three-ply, covered with silver paper, that acted as mirrors to increase the light on a subject.) We were filming away happily, when there was an almighty crash, and there was Pat on the coals, looking slightly bewildered, and sans reflector. He had neglected to see a bridge approaching! All he said was 'Pass me another one, will you?' I never had such an assistant as Pat Jackson. My favourite memory of him was on a later film *The Saving of Bill Blewett*. We had suddenly discovered, right out in the heart of Cornwall, and without transport, that we'd forgotten an essential 'prop'. Pat didn't hesitate. The usual crowd had gathered, including a yokel leaning on his bicycle. Pat whipped the bike from under him, with a 'Do you mind, sir?' in his impeccable public-school accent, and was off down the hill like a bomb. Shaking with laughter, we placated the yokel until Pat came puffing back, and his beaming 'I must say, sir, that was jolly decent of you' so mollified the bike-owner that he stuck around all afternoon.

After Beattock, we went on into Scotland to get the shots for the glorious rush that was the end of the journey. Travelling up and down the line with a camera eye, particularly in the dawn, dozens of lovely visuals presented themselves as the train thundered by. The covey of partridges taking off, the rabbits running for cover, with their white scuts aloft, the farm dogs making a race of it just for fun, and the early workers sleepily giving us a wave. To get some of these shots I went back to the little farm where I had run wild for two years. Something I found there moved me very much. It had been sold many years before to a battling couple with a small family. Although lovely, it was a poor hill farm, with barely a living in it. The most striking feature had been a grove of the most magnificent beech trees surrounding the steading. My mother, and later my father, had often been approached to sell them for timber, and had always refused. But they were worth a lot of money, and I felt sure I would find them gone. Yet, as I turned the familiar corner at the foot of the valley, there were the beeches in all their massive dignity. After the grand high tea and 'a wee dram' to celebrate my return, I told the farmer of my fears. He was indignant, and rather hurt. 'I wouldnae cut doon thon trees for aw the tea in Chiny. When I gang oot o' an evening tae smoke ma pipe, and think o' the wark like, I get a sort of comfort from thae trees. They're noble, ye see.' This was true aesthetic appreciation, so much more real than the inbred simperings of the so-called experts who bore you with their patronage on TV or the literary pages.

We went on to Glasgow from the Dumfriesshire farm, and I was shocked to get a message from Grierson to say that, apart from the studio interiors and the sound, we had no more money, and must stop shooting. But I wasn't finished! I had become fascinated with the engine—what is it that makes people so mad about railway steam engines?—and I wanted a coda at the end of the film, of the engine, still dirty and hot after its night's labour, being cleaned down, oiled and greased, and made ready for its next journey. We were staying in the most awful scruffy digs in Glasgow as it was, but now we couldn't even afford that.

The Post Office Accounts Department, bewildered by suddenly finding themselves landed with an unestablished section, manned by apparent idiots who had no idea how to handle money, had evolved a typical civil service method of estimating our travelling allowances. They looked at our salaries, and allocated us a 'grade' in the Post Office equivalent to them. Thus, as far as I can remember, I was on a par with a telephone linesman, first class. Jonah Jones and Chick Fowle were linesmen, second class, and God knows what Pat Jackson ranked. It didn't matter, of course, because we all mucked in together. But I can tell you telephone linesmen lived rough in those days.

The only thing to do was to descend on my mother, who was living in Edinburgh. She took the arrival of the little troupe in her stride, and made us very comfortable. We travelled daily in a guard's van to Glasgow, ate my mother's excellent sandwiches, and got the last shots without it costing a penny. When we got back, we found the sorting van interiors built and ready, and no-one seemed to notice we had been a week adrift.

The set of a whole railway carriage was an ambitious one for our tiny studio, but looked extremely authentic. Indeed, I imagine many people who have seen the film will not have realized that this sequence was done in the studio. The main problem was to get movement on it, to simulate the fact that the train was travelling at seventy miles an hour. We had none of the hydraulic aids or sets built on massive springs that the large studios use. So we had to show our ingenuity, as usual. Shaking the set was no good. It just rattled like a sideboard in a junction town. Moving the camera only made a wobbly camera movement. Knowing we would have train noise going on all through the sequence, we finally produced a simple solution. The real railway sorters manned the set, of course, and as they spent four days a week standing and balancing in trains, we just asked them to sway gently as they worked or talked, and this, plus one other trick, worked the effect perfectly. Beside each two or three sorters a string hung down from a ball fixed on the roof, to tie the bundles of letters as they were sorted. In every shot, if we could, we swayed this string, just enough to give a bit of movement. It was extraordinary how that tiny swinging motion, plus the sound, created the illusion of speed.

While I had been shooting, Wright and Cavalcanti had been cutting the film with the new editor McNaughton, and a marvellous job they were doing. Few non-film people realize what an enormous contribution a good editor makes to a picture. While admitting he cannot turn dross into gold, he can so alter a director's clumsy or tentative efforts as to make them almost unrecognizable. What he can do is to give tempo and emphasis. We all know that tunes picked out on one finger by some illiterate in Tin Pan Alley become lovely pieces of music when played by a skilled band. Somewhere along the line that tune, which, of course, had to have musical potential, was dissected, rearranged and orchestrated by the backroom boys. A film editor is an orchestrator. Just as the effect of a piece of music is utterly lost if it is played *fortissimo*, or too fast or too slow all the time, so a film must constantly change its pace to obtain its dramatic effects. In scripting or directing, of course, this is known and kept very much in mind. But the same scene is generally filmed from several angles, with long shots, medium shots and close shots. It is in his selection of these shots, their length and their juxtaposition, that the editor makes his tempo and his emphasis. A creative cutter is not necessarily restricted by what was in the script or what the director handed over. He can turn a scene inside out, or even more importantly, eliminate it altogether. This presupposes a close liaison and mutual confidence between editor and director which, all too often, does not occur. As I have said, film directors are the final egocentrics, and feel that their talents are God-given. Luckily, there is a *deus ex machina* in the producer, or films would never get finished.

As, obviously, Wright and Cavalcanti were much more skilled at editing than I was, I busied myself getting the background sounds. We took the sound-van out to places like Bletchley, and got all sorts of perspectives of the sound of the passing trains. We arranged with the railway for the trains to make different types of engine noise as they passed us, and we got a marvellous whistle, starting far away, rising to a shrieking crescendo as it passed us, and then dying away, that I swear has been used in every steam train film ever made since that time. We soon struck an enormous snag. We needed, of course, the sound of the travelling train as heard by the people on it. To get this we put our enormous sound-van onto a flat bogey behind a special train, and trundled up and down the line all one Sunday. (In these days of attaché-case sound systems, this must sound incredible.) Inside our private carriage, we could get the general sound all right, and variations caused by passing bridges, tunnels and the like. But our microphones were not selective enough to get the 'clickity-clack, clickity-clack' of the wheels as they crossed the joins in the rails. The general overall roar drowned this out. We tried everything, outside the window, inside with the windows closed, microphone on the roof, on the floor, all no good. We thought we'd solved it when somebody suggested dangling the mike down the open lavatory. Even then the roar drowned the clacks. We gave up in despair.

This was a major setback. The central sequence of the film depended on the trainee mail-dropper hearing and counting the 'clickity-clacks' or beats, as his instructor called them, before the pouch went out, and we intended bringing them up to dominate the sound as we held the close-up of his face counting. We tried all sorts of compromises in the cutting-room. We even cut the sound-track of the overall train noise into tiny sections and then joined them together again in a 'clickety-clack' pattern, hoping this would give the effect. It sounded like a series of hiccups.

Then somebody had a brilliant, simple idea. We would do it in model. Off we went to Bassett Lowke, the model train makers, and got a class-six engine, made to perfect scale. The model rails were also to scale. It was then a simple mathematical calculation to work out, as the joins in the full-size rails were twenty-six feet apart, where to file nicks in the model rails. Every three inches, shall we say? We knew the speed at which the trainee counted, from our picture of him, so we pushed our tiny train by hand backward and forwards on its section of line until we were in synchronism with the picture and then recorded it. It worked a treat. All we had to do was to marry this sound to the general noise of the train at speed, and we had got what we wanted.

This may sound too laborious and detailed for a moment in a short film, and only of interest to technically-minded people. I have put it down, because part of the reason for this exercise is to show the rather complacent technocrats of today what we were up against, and because the solving of that problem is an achievement ever present in my memories. Without that sound, the centre of a film that was to make my career would have completely failed. When I see the film again, I don't see the nervous trainee or his instructor. I see Pat Jackson's earnest face, sweating with concentration, pushing his toy train backwards and forwards, backwards and forwards, while I am beating time like a podgy metronome, and the sound man, deadpan as always, swings his microphone in unison.

Somebody suggested that Auden should write the commentary for the end part of the picture—in verse. It was not I who had the idea, and I wasn't particularly keen. I want to be utterly fair about all this, because when the film became one of the peaks of documentary achievement and a museum piece, there began the usual arguments from the analysts and the experts of who did what, and whose contribution was the most important. All I know is that I directed every foot of the picture. That is, I chose the visuals, showed the cast what to do, wrote the dialogue and, from Wright's notes, planned the overall shape of the film. The aesthetic highlights, that is, Auden's poetry, Britten's music and the overall editing, were the ideas and work of Wright and Cavalcanti, under Grierson. If anyone was ever to make an analysis of my films, he would see it all starting in *Night Mail*. I developed a capacity to portray ordinary people in dramatic form, yet at the same time make them appear completely natural on the screen. It was dramatic journalism, without the hysterics and exaggerations of the press. My jokes were awful, my dialogue flat. But it was real, and therefore successful, because the public will always recognize this reality. I don't think this is boasting, because, although I knew I could do this, I never quite knew how it came about. It was, perhaps, merely simplicity—not naïveté, which is only a knife-edge away, but poles apart. Cavalcanti paid me my greatest compliment when he said 'Harry Watt put the sweaty sock into documentary.'

Auden sat down to write his verse. Being at the GPO Film Unit, he had no pleasant, airy office, looking out on the children playing, and the old men dozing in the sun. He got a bare table at the end of a dark, smelly, noisy corridor. We were now bursting at the seams, and the last corner available was in what was inevitably known as 'the back passage'. It ran parallel with the theatre, where films were constantly being shown. At one end, a bunch of messenger boys played darts, wrestled, and brewed tea. At the other end, Auden, serene and uncomplaining, turned out some of the finest verse he has ever written. As it was a commentary, it had, of course, to fit the picture, so he would bring sections to us as he wrote them. When it did not fit, we just said so, and it was crumpled up and thrown into the waste-paper basket! Some beautiful lines and stanzas went into oblivion in this casual, ruthless way. Auden just shrugged, and wrote more. Wright and I can only remember one tiny lost fragment. Auden described the rounded lowland hills that you meet as you enter Scotland, as being 'heaped like slaughtered horses'—a tremendous visual image. The final commentary, the first part spoken by Stuart Legg at a great pace to match a rushing train, goes like this:

This is the night mail crossing the border,
Bringing the cheque and the postal order,
Letters for the rich, letters for the poor,
The shop at the corner and the girl next door.

Pulling up Beattock, a steady climb—
The gradient's against her but she's on time.
Past cotton grass and moorland boulder,
Shovelling white steam over her shoulder,
Snorting noisily as she passes
Silent miles of wind-bent grasses;
Birds turn their heads as she approaches,
Stare from the bushes at her blank-faced coaches;
Sheepdogs cannot turn her course,
They slumber on with paws across.
In the farm she passes no one wakes,
But a jug in the bedroom gently shakes.

By now the train has climbed Beattock Hill and the commentary
and visuals momentarily relax and draw their breath before the
train rushes down again into the industrial heart of Scotland.
John Grierson himself speaks this:

Dawn freshens, the climb is done.
Down towards Glasgow she descends
Towards the steam tugs, yelping down the glade of cranes
Towards the fields of apparatus, the furnaces
Set on the dark plain like gigantic chessmen.
All Scotland waits for her;
In the dark glens, beside the pale-green sea lochs,
Men long for news.

Again the commentary matches the speed of the train.

Letters of thanks, letters from banks,
Letters of joy from the girl and boy,
Receipted bills and invitations
To inspect new stock or visit relations,
And applications for situations,
And timid lovers' declarations,
And gossip, gossip from all the nations,
News circumstantial, news financial,
Letters with holiday snaps to enlarge in
Letters with faces scrawled on the margin.
Letters from uncles, cousins and aunts,

Letters to Scotland from the South of France,
Letters of condolence to Highlands and Lowlands,
Notes from overseas to the Hebrides;
Written on paper of every hue,
The pink, the violet, the white and the blue;
The chatty, the catty, the boring, adoring,
The cold and official and the heart's outpouring,
Clever, stupid, short and long,
The typed and the printed and the spelt all wrong.

Finally, against visuals of the main cities of Scotland in the early morning light the commentary is again taken up by John Grierson.

Thousands are still asleep
Dreaming of terrifying monsters
Or a friendly tea beside the band at Cranston's or Crawford's;
Asleep in working Glasgow, asleep in well-set Edinburgh,
Asleep in Granite Aberdeen.
They continue their dreams
But shall wake soon and long for letters.
And none will hear the postman's knock
Without a quickening of the heart,
For who can bear to feel himself forgotten?

The music was the next problem, so one day Cavalcanti said to me, 'There's this boy, he is, I think, very clever. Maybe you should show him your film. I think he could do something about the music.' I asked 'What's his name?' Cav answered, 'Benjamin Britten—he is very young, but he will be very good.' So, rather nervously, into our theatre came this shy, soft-spoken kid, with close-curled blond hair, and a pale and sensitive face. For some reason I was alone. I knew nothing about music, but, as usual, had decided views on it, so I started right in 'The music has got to fit the picture, you understand, absolutely fit to a split-second. Also, I want it to be rhythmic, to go with the beat of the train. I've got a record here . . .' And, believe it or not, I then ran an old-time jazz record to Benjamin Britten to make my point! It wasn't 'Shuffle Off To Buffalo' but something like that. He didn't bat an eyelid, and merely com-

94

mented on the extraordinary technical skill there was in jazz. I had the grace to say that I only played it to demonstrate the kind of beat I wanted, and he relaxed as we ran the cutting copy of the film, which he liked very much. We broke it to him later that he could only have eight musicians and that his fee would be about ten pounds! It was one of Britten's first commissioned works, and the music he did for us showed all the enormous potential that Cavalcanti had spotted.

There was one amusing little postscript to the shooting of *Night Mail*. Seeing it with music and commentary, we decided we needed some extra shots of the engine, plus big close-ups of wheels, pistons, and so on, to cut in here and there to increase the feeling of speed—so back I went to my railway contact man, the bowler-hatted director, who had by now, no doubt under our influence, become quite a snappy dresser. He wore a soft hat at a jaunty angle, and had even been seen in flannel bags. He was, as always, eager to help, but when I told him that I wanted two trains running parallel, but with a line in between them, he nearly collapsed. It meant that one of the trains would be going in the wrong direction, as it were. The organization must have been enormous, but in three weeks, early one Sunday morning, Chick and Jonah, Pat and I climbed onto a very low bogey, towed by a tank engine, and waited for the other train to appear. Then the railway produced their gift package. Into the platform parallel with us came, not our faithful class six engine, but the railway's newest, most spanking, chromium-plated monster! Old Stone—yes, that was his name, I've remembered now, we gave him such a dog's life he deserves a credit—was so pleased with his surprise for us, and so eager to hear our exclamations of admiration and delight, that we hadn't the heart to tell him that we now couldn't take the wonderful master shots we had planned, and all he would see of his juggernaut would be tiny details.

As a farewell gift, I sent him a book on film continuity. I never got an acknowledgment.

The film was 'dubbed', that is, all the sounds, dialogue, music, commentary and background sounds were all mixed together on one sound-track, and the 'married print' was produced, where the sound and picture are on one piece of film. As I was still a junior member of the organization, I had not been consulted about the 'credits', which are the names that generally irritate the public at the beginning of a film. I had better explain about credits. To us, in the film business, they are our life-blood, our bread-and-butter, our reward for years of dedication and application. They mean jobs, mentions in anthologies, triumphs over rivals, or, in the gamble that is the excitement of it all, carrying the can for a flop. In commercial films particularly, when somebody applies for a job he says 'I had a credit on so-and-so', or 'I was only second assistant, but they were so pleased with my work they gave me a credit'. So I beg the public, on films or television, to bear with those names. If they see 'Special boots by Joe Smithers' or 'Punch-up arranged by Charley Staircase', it may mean that Joe's or Charley's family eat next week.

When I saw the credits of *Night Mail*, I was shocked. The main credit was 'Produced by Basil Wright and Harry Watt'. But I hadn't produced it, I'd directed it! I was by now determined to be a film director, and a good one, and I wanted this stated up on the screen for this film. Wright was my senior—he already had *Song of Ceylon* under his belt—and deserved the larger credit. But, even if it was in letters half the size, I wanted 'Directed by Harry Watt'.

I set off in a fury to search Grierson out on the small-holding he'd recently acquired in Kent. This was another of Grierson's amusing rackets. He had fruit-trees, strawberry beds and so on, but no-one to work them. So all of us were asked down for a pleasant day in the country, and ended up working our tail off in the fields. We always got a feed and a good drink, and it was rather fun, but, as usual, we were being pleasantly exploited.

I demanded that I have my name separate from Wright's, in letters as tiny as Grierson cared, and he refused point-blank. My only answer would have been to resign, and, of course, I didn't. Grierson, one of the world's greatest salesmen, double-talked me round, and I ended up working in the garden. But I never forgave him this. It may seem a minor point to non-film people, but when the picture became famous, those credits have created endless bickering as to who contributed what to it.

The film had an immediate *succès d'estime*, but the impact it made at first was comparatively small. It had its world première at the Arts Theatre in Cambridge, but the only

Above: My father, complete with buttonhole, white bowler and spats, with some Glasgow worthies in 1915

Right: My mother and I at my father's graveside in Kilmun, Argyllshire, around 1930

Pat Jackson directing *Western Approaches* in 1943-4   John Grierson

The gibbet on the side of the track just after the train has collected a mail bag (*Night Mail*, 1936)

My flash car used as camera dolly while shooting *The Saving of Bill Blewett*. The three foreground figures are Cavalcanti, me in check shirt, and Pat Jackson
Overleaf: The first balloon barrage crew in action at the Forth Bridge (*Squadron 992*)

Bill Blewett in *The Saving of Bill Blewett* (1936)

Mattie Mair as the skipper in *North Sea* (1938)

London Can Take It (1941). The young man on the back of the cart above is Henry Spiro, later to be killed while in the Navy

The final briefing in *Target for Tonight* (1941)

Above and below: London Can Take It

Vaagso in flames, 1942
Nine Men (1943)

London showing I can remember was three days at a newsreel cinema in Charing Cross Road. Certainly my life was unaffected and nobody offered me a job, or anything like that, although I think I got a raise to five quid a week.

4

Grierson now started a film paper *World Film News* and it was pretty fair chaos from the word go. I was only on the fringes, but, as usual, we all had to work on it. We knew nothing of magazine production, but Grierson decided that we must prepare the first 'dummy' ourselves. The dummy is a mock-up edition, with the articles, pictures and so on, roughly printed and then stuck onto loose pages to give an idea of what the final product will look like. It turned out to be a much more difficult and skilled job than any of us had imagined. Grierson demanded enormous headlines, about the size the *Daily Mirror* has when it gets a scoop. But he also wanted to use the long words he delighted in, like 'horizons' or 'leadership'. These, of course, just would not fit, so the first number became a ghastly jigsaw of big black letters, with little bits of normal print tucked away around the bottom of the page. Considerably chastened, Grierson engaged a German refugee, who had run a similar magazine in Berlin, as editor; Vicky, the to-be-famous cartoonist, then a shy, half-starved-looking youth, to do the illustrations, and Esmond Romilly as advertising manager. He was a fascinating character, only about eighteen, but incredibly sophisticated for his age. His mother was Winston Churchill's sister-in-law, his father a bewildered, stuffy colonel. Esmond had been expelled from his public school for defending masturbation in the school magazine. He then lived by his wits for two years, selling silk stockings door-to-door—at seventeen, with his public-school accent, he called himself Captain Romilly to impress the wretched housewives—then got involved in some dubious second-hand car deals, but refused to have anything to do with his family, who had tried to get the police to control him. He was amusing, charming, utterly carefree, and not very good at his job. Eventually, when this was pointed out to him, he knocked the editor down, and left. He was next heard of in

Spain, then, of course, in the throes of its Civil War. He had with him, of all people, Jessica Mitford, one of the famous sisters, an equally influential and important family. As the girl was reported to be pregnant, it is said that a British destroyer went in to pick them up. At any rate, they both suddenly appeared again, now married, and living in a slum house in the East End of London, where we had some monumental drunken parties. They suddenly went to America and eventually were reported running a club or something like that in Florida. I had forgotten all about him until one evening, after the world war had broken out, I was having a drink in the little back bar of the old Café Royal, which had become our hang-out. At a table in one corner was a noisy bunch of Canadian Air Force sergeants, arguing loudly in raw, twangy accents. I looked across irritably, and then looked again. I went over to the one that had seemed the roughest of the lot and asked 'Aren't you Esmond Romilly?' He looked up at me with the old cheeky grin, left his seat and came back to the bar, saying as he did so, in his usual impeccable public school voice 'How are you, old boy? How nice to see you'. I, of course, said 'Why, in Christ's name, are you talking that incredibly awful imitation Canadian?' He was rather hurt, and explained that his pals couldn't understand him when he talked normally, so he had adopted their accent. He was play-acting, as usual. It turned out that he'd become ashamed of lazing in the Florida sun, and had gone across to Canada and joined up. He had obviously not used any of the enormous influence he could have drawn upon, because he was a sergeant rear-gunner, the lowest flying-rank, and the most dangerous job in Bomber Command. After his drink with me, he rejoined his mates, and as I left, I heard his phoney twang start up again. Two days later he was killed. I don't suppose he was twenty-one.

It was in that same Café Royal bar that we behaved so abominably to Dylan Thomas. We all knew he was brilliant, but we had considerable creative conceits ourselves, and so were not overly impressed. The truth is, he was a cadger. We'd see him come in, whisper 'Look out, there's that awful little Welsh shit' and close our ranks. If he managed to get past our phalanx of backs, we would stand him a drink, but it nearly always ended up with him making a touch. So much has been written about Dylan Thomas that very few stories remain untold. My favourite story belongs to Jeevers Wynn-Jones, a famous Welsh sports commentator. In his early days, Jeevers acted as a 'stringer', that is a free-lance reporter, for various London papers. He was to send in a report to a Sunday paper of an important cricket match, but, trying to cover too many events, he failed to make the ground in time. The only person he found there when he arrived was Dylan Thomas, a keen cricket fan, but blind drunk as usual. Jeevers tried to get his story from Dylan, who insisted on phoning it through to London himself. It was a question of no story, no pay, so, in considerable trepidation, he agreed. Dylan disappeared into a telephone box, was watched by Jeevers with growing horror as he gesticulated and mouthed, and then fell out of the box with 'That'll cost you a double.' Next day, Jeevers got a message from the sports editor, congratulating him on his cricket report, and asking indignantly why, if he could put such imagination into this article, his others were so pedestrian! Poor old Jeevers had to think up occasional magical word-pictures for years.

World Film News was by now functioning reasonably smoothly, and Grierson sent me out on my first writing assignment. I was to interview Max Miller, the top comedian of the time, famous for his machine-gun non-stop patter, and topping the bill at the Palladium. Considering I didn't take a note and there were, of course, no tape-recorders in those days, I got quite a good impression of his patter. Grierson was delighted with it, gave me a byline and front-page spread, and announced that I would do a weekly series of interviews with top actors and actresses, beginning with Charles Laughton. I refused point-blank. I've always been embarrassed by this little episode, because the reasons I gave for refusing were bumptious and conceited for a film-maker hardly out of swaddling clothes. I actually said that, as I intended to be an important director, and meet these people on equal terms, I thought that pestering them on behalf of a tiny magazine would affect my career! I was so inexperienced that I did not realize that film people, and actors particularly, will fall over themselves for any publicity, and that I would, in fact, have made myself many useful contacts for this imaginary future. When I worked with Laughton later on, and told him this story, he rightly said 'You *were* a bloody young fool.'

Grierson had to accept my decision, as working for *World Film News* was extra-mural, as it were, and without pay. It wasn't long before he put me in my place by telling me I had to make a film for the Post Office Savings Bank, to promote and encourage saving. To me, this was a ghastly assignment. Organized saving seemed like organized religion, and equally repulsive. But it is interesting that I took it, as we always did, as a job that had to be done, and it was just up to us to find an angle, a 'gimmick' if you like, to make such subjects filmic. Now that the British documentary movement has been written about so much as an original and revolutionary art-form, I have often tried to explain to modern highbrows that we did not consider ourselves as artists, but as technicians or reporters on film. Anybody who had talked of 'waiting for the mood', or 'needing the right atmosphere to create', or any of that sort of crap, would have soon got the old heave-ho. We occasionally found marvellous subjects in the extraordinary ramifications of the GPO, but, more often than not, had to fit into their overall planning, and then astonish them with our interpretations. To their eternal credit, they generally liked our surprises.

Somehow or other I managed to think up a story about saving that involved fishing boats and fishermen. I would have twisted every story I ever wrote onto the sea, if I could have been ingenious enough. For some mysterious atavistic reason, it is only commercial fishing I am interested in. No skimming the waters for me, just plough the bottom with a dirty great net. I still own a fishing-boat in Scotland, and it is the gamble I adore. One day make a little fortune, next day catch your net on a wreck, and lose the bloody lot.

The story I wrote was extremely simple. Two fishermen anchor their boat off the harbour to go ashore and buy some stores. In a sudden squall, their anchor drags, and their uninsured craft is wrecked. They have to get work, so one goes to sea as a deck-hand on a big trawler, and the other, who is married, stays back in the village and works in a quarry. The married one likes his drink, so, on day, pinches five bob from the family teapot, and sneaks towards the pub. Unfortunately for him, just as he reaches it he sees his wife coming, so he avoids her by dodging into the nearest doorway, which happens to be the village hall. To his considerable consternation, he finds a meeting of the local Savings Committee in progress. They welcome him warmly, rather like the Salvation Army receiving a lost soul, and, after a pompous talk on the virtues of saving, ask our fisherman how much he will start his account with. In front of all those local eyes, he knows he's done for, and plumps down his all. When he gets home, his wife has found out about the missing money, and starts in on him. With a flourish, he produces his Post Office book, and astonishes her with a somewhat garbled version of the pious balderdash he had been forced to listen to at the village hall. Knowing him, his wife realizes there's something very smelly about the whole thing, but is delighted that he's going to start saving.

The two men go on working, but keep longing, as only people who have owned their own boat do, to sail together again as their own masters. Suddenly in the little harbour, the ideal fishing boat comes up for sale. It is owned by an old, bad-tempered character, who thinks he can get more money for it if he sells it to 'foreigners' as a 'yat'. Our two chaps get together, and find they have saved £50 between them. They offer it as a down payment on the new boat, but the old fisherman turns them down flat. They accuse him of being a traitor to the village, to fishermen, to his boat. They tell him that he couldn't lift his head in the neighbourhood if lousy amateurs tart up the boat that had provided the living for him and his family, with white paint and chromium. The old boy is shaken by their arguments, but tantalizes them for a while by showing a series of dreadful tourists over the boat. Eventually, he lets our chaps have her, and they sail off to the fishing grounds, and get a great catch.

Such a corny story wouldn't get past the third assistant scenario editor in provincial television today, but somehow Grierson bought it, and it is astonishing to find it described in Paul Rotha's *The Film Till Now* as 'a film that was to influence others in the movement and give a line of development towards the use of story and actors that meant the progressive dropping of the "unseen" commentator, and consequently the greater use of natural sound.' Put simply, it was the first story documentary film.

I now had to find a location to fit the story. With my new,

self-appointed position as an embryo maestro, I had acquired—for £40—a magnificent car. It was a very old open Chrysler, with huge chrome exhausts coming out of each side of the bonnet. When I operated the cutout, it made a noise like the Concorde. I had also acquired an equally impressive ulster overcoat down to my heels in a very bright russet colour. The Watt clan had been seen around in this colour for almost a generation, owing to one of my father's eccentricities. One year, on his farm, he believed he was being swindled over the price of his wool, so he sought out a tiny woollen mill somewhere in the border country, and ordered all his wool to be turned into tweed. It was superb cloth, but he had forgotten to specify the colour, so it all turned up russet red. Bales of it had been handed out all over Scotland, and my mother sent me the very last bit. The whole ensemble must have made me look like a Middle European spy in a B-picture, but I was extremely pleased with myself.

I was cut down to size in the lovely little fishing village of Pittenweem, in Fifeshire. I roared up in my flash car, got out in my flash coat, and started making the gestures with my hands I'd seen movie directors doing, that is, putting my thumbs together to make a rough rectangle, and moving them about to pretend they were the camera. I wasn't quite sure what this was going to tell me, but I thought it looked good. I was watched by one solemn small boy, who followed me with that wondering, unblinking stare that children have. At last I condescended to notice him, and nodded down at him with 'Hullo, son.' Without changing his expression at all, he replied 'Hullo, fatty.'

In my search for a fishing village location, I finally landed up in Mousehole in Cornwall, on a stinking wet day. As usual, I was supposed to report to the postmaster, but I thought a drink was indicated first. There was only one other chap in the pub, a thick-set, ruddy faced typical fisherman. We got chatting and I asked him what he'd have. 'Double rum' he says, pretty smartly. So we had rums, and many more rums, and eventually I just managed to get off my stool, and, enunciating very carefully, said 'I must go and find the postmaster.' My friend then climbed off his stool, held tight onto the counter and announced 'I am the postmaster!' That was the beginning of a long association and a great friendship. My drinking companion was

Bill Blewett, who eventually gave his name to the title of my film, played the lead, and featured in many other pictures.

What incredible self-confidence we had—or bloody cheek perhaps—in setting off in a clapped-out Chrysler, with a unit of four and a thousand pounds, to make a half-hour all-dialogue story film, with no professional actors. I used to think of this sometimes when I was forced to take out a unit of sixty people to get, say, a couple of shots of someone jumping on a motorbike. Pat Jackson was the same eager assistant, Jonah Jones the cameraman, but the new twist was that Pat had an assistant! Well, sort of. I had done a real exploratory deal. I needed a young Cornishman to play Bill Blewett's partner. Of all people, that old reprobate George Noble the cameraman turned up with a brother-in-law, very handsome, genuine Cornish accent, and mad to get into films. So I made him second lead actor, but also second assistant when he wasn't acting. It worked extremely well, and Joe Jago is now a top film photographer.

I learnt a great deal shooting *The Saving of Bill Blewett*, because our only real professional, Cavalcanti, moved in and helped me when I started to get into a mess. From him I found that filming a story was quite different from our usual general sort of atmospheric shooting. Your audience is interested in your principal artists only and, through them, follows the story. When I started shooting, I would, for instance, have long scenes with my actors mingling with a crowd of others, all the same size on the screen. I imagined that the viewers would pick out our characters easily enough. But this is not so. If they have to search the crowd for the principals, there is an immediate impatience, and you lose the concentration that you must have to hold an audience. You watch in the next film you see. There will be a flash of, say, Oxford Street, and in a couple of seconds there are your actors walking along, or looking into a shop window. So they're going to do something interesting, and you wait to see what it is. I also learnt about continuity in dialogue scenes. Continuity can mean that a character must be wearing the same trousers when he walks out of the hall and appears in the garden. But by continuity of dialogue I mean the mechanics whereby people talk to each other on the screen. I imagine that everyone knows that close-ups are shot separately, that is, if two characters are shouting at each other and the head of each in turn fills the screen, each close-up is a separate shot, with the other actor standing beside the camera as an eye-line to talk to. Well, if actor A shouts left of camera, then actor B *must* shout right of camera, otherwise the impression is, when the two shots are put together in the editing, that they are not shouting at each other, but in opposite directions. Again, if actor A moves out of the camera frame—that is, what the lens sees—from left to right in order to embrace actress B, actress B must move out of frame right to left to meet him, otherwise she will look as though she is going to embrace the wall behind her. This becomes second nature to feature film people, but it got me in awful muddles, and I brought my wife down as unofficial continuity girl. Of course, the way we worked, she also provided the lunches, acted as an extra in the crowd scenes, controlled the rubber-neckers, carried the cables in the tracking shots, and generally worked like hell.

I also learnt from Cavalcanti the gentle art of faking, because, of course, ninety per cent of cinema is faked, in some way or other. When the sun moved off a scene, as it always seems to do at the crucial moment, he pointed out that a white fisherman's cottage round the corner, in full sun, exactly matched the one I was filming against, and all I had to do was move my actors thirty yards, place them in the same juxtaposition they were in before the shadows came, and carry on. To people trained in pure realism, this conception that all you needed to show was the camera eye—that is, what the lens takes in, took a bit of learning. You must realize that if you have, say, a thirty-yard gap between two enormous factories, but this gap looks out over the most beautiful countryside, you can place two lovers in front of the camera, just cut out the factories in your lens, and let them talk of how wonderful it is to be alone in this blissful wilderness. The viewers never conceive that there could be anything except more beautiful countryside all round, and if the locals spot it, they just think how bloody smart you were, and tell their friends to go and have a look.

We needed cottage interiors in the script, but our film wasn't fast enough to get satisfactory results in real cottages, so Cavalcanti showed me another continental trick, that I used several times later on. We found a ruined cottage overlooking the harbour. We gutted it, removed the roof, and redecorated it inside as a typical fisherman's home. We then put gauze all across the roof, which gave a lovely even light, and cut out harsh shadows. With a few supplementary lamps, we got a perfect exposure, with the enormous added advantage that we could see the real harbour beyond, and match exterior and interior action.

Everything was going fine, when Grierson dropped a ridiculous bombshell. I got a message to telephone him, and when I did so, I was astonished when he started 'I hear you've got your wife with you?' I said 'Yes, and very useful too.' He then said 'She must leave at once!' I couldn't believe I had heard him right. He knew my wife as a bright, intelligent, active person, who had a long experience of show business. When I asked him his reasons, he went into one of his long double-talk spiels about creative people not allowing their concentration to be dissipated by personal problems or domestic associations. This, while he was working his own wife into the ground typing out his endless articles, lectures, reports, talks and criticisms. He ended up by ordering me to send my wife away and, to my shame, I agreed. But that was the final lump of clay on my god's feet. All right, so he'd given me my chance, saved me at the crucial moment from being a drifter, but I'd given him in turn absolute devotion and loyalty, and earned my keep. The fact that, at this stage, when we were apparently grown-up, he could be so narrow, so stupidly Calvinistic, so dictatorial, scunnered me, as we Scots say. We were soon to go our separate ways, and this episode made me not too unhappy about it.

Bill Blewett ended on a wonderful Pat Jackson, the-eagerest-beaver-of-them-all, note. As I explained in the résumé of the story, our two fishermen had to sail off in their newly-bought boat, and make a fine first catch. To get this scene, we hired a fully equipped boat for a day, for the enormous sum—in our budget—of £15. We set off for Land's End in marvellous sun and shot long-lines, that is, about a mile of heavy line with a baited hook every six feet. We filmed Bill and Joe Jago baiting and shooting the lines, waited two hours, and started to haul. We were getting a tremendous catch of large conger eels—very exciting for the camera—when down comes the fog! There was nothing else to do but to bring in the rest of the lines and grope our way homeward. It was about ten at night when we got back to harbour, and, after everyone had cleared off, Pat and I debated desperately what we would do, as we reckoned we couldn't afford the boat for another day. The eels in the hold were still alive, if pretty moribund. Pat suddenly said he'd got the solution. We'd keep the eels alive overnight by sinking them in a box, hire the boat for a couple of quid to go just outside the harbour, stick the eels back on the hooks, and bob would be your uncle! That was great, but it was now dark, we had no box to keep the eels in, and, on examination, they were not going to be with us much longer. Pat rushed off like a bullet. He soon found the local carpenter, very drunk, in a pub, and somehow—only Pat would know how—persuaded him to go to his workshop and make a box. By midnight we had an enormous coffin on our hands which Pat and I, looking like Burke and Hare, carried down through the sleeping village to the harbour. We shoved the eels in, and then launched it on the water. It floated beautifully, but the eels might as well have stayed in the hold. It was so light, that not a drop of water wetted the bottom—or the eels!

Naturally, Pat was not defeated. Ignoring my despairing curses, he kept saying 'Don't worry, old boy, I'll fix it' as he scrabbled about in the bowels of the boat. He suddenly reappeared humping a 56lb iron weight, used as ballast. 'This'll sink her all right' he said as he dropped it into the box. It did, in a way. It went straight through the bottom of the box, and our eels, suddenly less lethargic, swam happily back to Land's End!

We compromised the last sequence with a botched up marriage of what we had got before the fog and Bill and Joe landing a borrowed catch at the fish market, and it worked reasonably well. This business of compromise bedevils every film-maker—certainly in my league. There may be geniuses who refuse to do it; they generally end up washing dishes, or bankrupting their backers. If one accepts film as an art, then it must surely be the only one that is, almost invariably, being debased from the moment the idea is conceived. Apart from having to have monied support, one is usually dependent on self-centred actors, bored technicians, and a morass of technical and mechanical reproduction, which invariably means failure at one stage or other. One sets off on every new production believing that the actors are Olivier and Garbo, that the sun will always shine, that the camera and sound will never break down, that even the second assistant wardrobe mistress is a genius, and inevitably, inexorably, on the very first day, the whole bloody thing blows up in your face. Your beautiful graphs, your cross-indexed schedule, your plan to show them back at the front office, is up the goddam spout, and you're at it until midnight working out what the hell you'll do next day. I honestly reckon that in all the films I've made, the ones I realized about fifty per cent of my original imaginings were the successes—let's forget the others. If I was summoned before some celestial critic's circle, and asked what I had contributed, I would only offer about half a dozen sequences—not films, sequences, that is to say, moments—as anything I could see again and not regret. A bit from *Night Mail*, *North Sea* and *Squadron 992*, *The Overlanders*, *Where No Vultures Fly*, and maybe *People Like Maria* are all I can think of.

Bill Blewett was edited and handed over to the Savings Bank. I suppose they liked it reasonably well, although I imagine, in their innermost hearts, they would have preferred something with a character like Lord Kitchener pointing out of the screen and saying 'Your Country Needs You To Save'. But everyone in the Post Office had by now been conditioned by Grierson to believe that they were patrons of the arts. This is, of course, the easiest form of flattery to be successful. Tell anyone that he is sensitive and appreciative of true values, etcetera, and you've got a sponsor—except in Wardour Street, of course.

Apart from learning a lot of new techniques, the most valuable thing I got out of *Bill Blewett* was Bill Blewett himself —one of the great British characters. He was really a fisherman born and bred, and the Post Office was run by his lovely wife, Hetty. He was the perfect actor, because he was utterly unself-conscious and relaxed, and oozed personality. I brought him to London for the first time, and when I asked him what he wanted to see I imagined he'd say the Maritime Museum at Greenwich. He said Fortnum and Mason's, London's most exclusive shop! He had read about it, apparently, and the exotic foods from all over the world intrigued him. So, dressed in his blue woollen fisherman's jersey and a cloth cap, off we go to Fortnums. When we go in, Bill marches straight up to the floor-walker at the door—they all wear black morning coats and striped trousers, as though they're just off to a reception at the Palace—stuck out his hand, and said, in thick Cornish, 'I'm Bill Blewett, from Mousehole [pronounced Muzzle], how are they treating you 'ere?' The floor-walker was so astonished that he only mumbled 'Oh, very well'. Bill went on, in what only can be described as his regal manner, 'I'm glad to hear that, I've heard say that some of these posh places don't treat their workers that good. I've read a lot about this 'ere shop, will you show me around a bit?' To make a long story short, such was Bill's utter self-confidence and personality, that he was taken round every-where, behind the scenes, into the inner sanctums, asked his opinion of the fish department—he expressed his disappoint-ment that tinned Cornish pilchards were not on sale, which they promised to rectify immediately—and was finally seen off by three floor-walkers. I can vouch for all this, because I followed round like an equerry. When we got outside all Bill said was 'They seem 'appy, 'Arry, that's the main thing', and never referred to Fortnums again.

After delivering *Bill Blewett*, I don't remember seeing it again. This surprises a lot of people, but I imagine novelists seldom re-read their books, or painters follow-up and gaze at their work after it's been sold. We had no commercial exploitation to bother about. With feature films, we were sent round the country, after the London Trade Show and Press Show, to try and sell the film to the provinces. Surrounded by a gaggle of public relations people, the producer and director, with perhaps a contract actor or actress, we would plod from one showing to another, each usually followed by a dreadful lunch and a speech from the local mayor, who invariably seemed to start by saying 'I never go to the pictures myself', and then tell us what we should put in them.

* * * * *

Before I could be allocated to a new subject, the big split in the documentary movement suddenly took place. Grierson announced that he was leaving the GPO, taking with him most of the senior members of the Unit. It was put out that he had conceived a brilliant new idea. The continued frustra-tion of making films that were praised by the best critics, internationally admired, accepted as a unique new film approach, yet denied a reasonable showing by the commercial cinema, made Grierson decide to try and take films to the twenty-odd million people who never went to the pictures. In fact, to create what became known as the non-theatrical circuit, showing films in schools, exhibitions, village halls, or to interested groups wherever a projector could be set up. Cavalcanti and I reacted violently against this new idea. I don't imagine now that Grierson wanted us with him, but I finally finished any possibility when I said, in my diplomatic way, that 'I didn't want to make films whose main function would be to allow old ladies to rest their tired feet'.

Cav and I were equally frustrated by the attitude of the commercial distributors, but we still believed that unless we could beat this barrier, we would not have succeeded in the original conception of what we had set out to do. We were convinced that, unless our films, with their message of the dignity of the ordinary man, could compete with commercial film on its own ground, that is, in the cinemas where people paid to see and enjoy them, we would have failed. This meant, of course, that our films must be entertainment, a dirty word amongst the intellectuals. All of the people who stayed on at the GPO, with the infinite conceit of the completely dedicated, went beyond this. We believed that, unless we persuaded the entrenched and utterly reactionary British cinema that the realist approach to film stories and film making was actually better entertainment than theirs, we had also failed. This was, at that time, tilting at windmills. The coming of war was to prove us right.

Grierson was proved right, too. From his propagandizing, proselytizing, reporting and sheer hard selling, documentary units sprang up in big business and throughout the Empire, usually manned by his nominees. His final and fitting memorial is the National Film Board of Canada, which he created and headed throughout the war, and which is the only active and important centre for the production of realist films left today.

Another facet of Grierson's flair was his capacity to spot ability in the oddest people. There was Len Lye, a gangling half-New Zealander half-Chinese, with a voice like a saw and a grin that split his face like a Hallowe'en turnip, who drifted in with a really original film idea. He was the first person in the world to interpret sounds on film in terms of colour and shapes. What he did was take plain sound-track—that is, clear 35mm film with the sound recorded down one edge—and paint by hand on the film, frame by frame, coloured designs to match the music. Each frame had to be different, and when you realize that there are 16 frames to a foot of film and that 90 feet of film goes through a projector every minute, you can get some idea of the painstaking work involved. Len was utterly broke—I have never known him otherwise—but had persuaded somebody to record a bright, brassy rhumba for him. To the considerable danger of his neighbours as, of course, it was all inflammable nitrate film in those days, he had started his experiments in a bed-sitter in Notting Hill Gate, matching the vibrations he could see on the sound-track. His technique is very difficult to describe, but to almost each note, dots, triangles, rectangles, circles, or abstract designs shot about the screen, increasing, decreasing, mingling, changing shape, changing colour and always synchronizing with the music. It was tremendously exciting fun, and it was brand new. It has been copied and cribbed many times, including Walt Disney's *Fantasia*, but none have had the spontaneous gaiety of Len Lye's first productions, *Rainbow Dance* and *Colour Box*.

Somehow Grierson wangled £500 to finance him, but this had to be justified. So, at the end of Len's first film, rhumbaing around like mad amongst the whorls and whirligigs, appeared and disappeared the words 'Post Early in the Day'. This always got a roar of surprise and laughter from audiences, and was a marvellous piece of propaganda.

Then there were two young Scots, Norman McLaren and Stewart McAllister. McLaren was a lissom, bright kid from Glasgow Arts School who improved on Len Lye's original idea with tiny figures on a Daliesque background, and whose anti-war cartoon *Neighbours*, made in Canada, where he is now one of the heads of the Canadian National Film Board, has become world-famous. McAllister was a very different character—exceedingly scruffy, very hairy, very rough, and completely anarchistic. He developed into a really great editor, and he and I became close friends when we worked on pictures together. To prove this, and to show the easy-going communism that existed at the unit, the following encounter or something similar often took place after the running of my rushes.

McAllister: What am ah supposed to dae wi' that load of crap?
Watt: Cut it, you Scots clot.
McAllister: Ah can tell ye ten places where it'll no' cut.
Watt: If you can't cut that, you'd better go back to scratching your arse in a Glasgow close-mouth.
McAllister: Aweel, ah'll just hae to try, but (pointing fiercely) ah'm no promisin' anything.
Watt: Piss off.

I suppose only men can see what love there is in such a conversation.

Then Bill Coldstream—now Sir William Coldstream, CBE, if you please, and formerly Principal of the Slade School of Fine Art—came and went, another intellectual who, I imagine, regretted his flirtation with films. I remember him as a horribly harassed young man, who worried so much about the shooting of his only film, *The Making of a King's Stamp*, that he could barely cast a shadow by the time he had finished.

He became very forgetful, and once mislaid, at the studio, a stamp album worth many thousands of pounds loaned from the Royal Collection. An electrician found it, and, having heard of its value, wrapped it up carefully before handing it back to the Keeper of the Stamps, or whatever he was called, who had brought it down. It wasn't until the old boy started to pack the album away that it was realized that it was wrapped in the *Daily Worker*! We all hoped he had a good read when he got back to the Palace.

The film was about the whole process of producing a commemorative stamp, from the rough designs through to the final printing. The artist involved in Coldstream's chaotic efforts was Barnett Friedman, a lovely man. Immensely talented and very famous, he retained his real Cockney accent, looked like a caricature of an East-End Jew, and revelled in it. He loved telling stories against himself, like the one when he was elected to the Carlton Club, a very select establishment in London's St James'. He hailed a taxi and said 'The Carlton Club—and 'urry.' The driver said 'The Carlton Sporting Club, Hackney, guv?' Barnett replied indignantly 'Naiow, the posh one—dahn St James' '. The cabby looked at him incredulously and said, 'Wot, you?'

The unusual aftermath of that film, which was an honest, straightforward job, was that for years it got an enormous distribution. It was, apparently, the only film ever made about stamps, and philatelic societies all over the world kept showing it.

With Grierson's departure, I suddenly became a senior, and Cavalcanti and I soon found ourselves, for a time, bogged down with administration and desk-work, but we managed to get young Pat Jackson launched as a director on a film describing the delivery of letters in the Fens called *Horsey Mail*, and then set about looking for the subject to justify our boast that documentary films could be sold commercially.

We found it in the Post Office ship-to-shore radio service. All around our coasts, radio stations keep constant contact with the ships of the world. In any crisis at sea, the whole rescue operation is controlled and monitored through these stations, and they can, and do, order the air to be cleared to enable the vital messages to be heard. Every winter, particularly amongst the fishing communities of the North, fearful dramas are recorded in the simple terse messages going back and forth from some dying ship to the Post Office telephonists. The story of one ship, its crew, and their battle to survive, would be our answer to Grierson.

I went off to Aberdeen to write the script. There was no plot, just a straightforward account, taken from the records of the Post Office and shipping companies, of how a rather elderly, coal-burning trawler leaves on a routine voyage, gets hit by a freak wave which rolls her over so much that the coal in the bunkers shifts to one side, thus giving her a dangerous list and choking her pumps. Just as she is beginning to report this, her aerial carries away, so that the authorities know there is a life and death crisis, but do not know exactly where, or how bad it is likely to become. For forty-eight hours, in radio silence and appalling weather, the crew of the trawler battle to stay alive, and only when they've beaten their own very immediate problems of survival, do they mend their aerial, and report that they are still afloat. Meantime, based on the meagre information they had received, the radio stations have been trying to contact ships in the approximate vicinity, getting salvage tugs organized, and keeping a twenty-four hours' listening watch for any sudden signal. On the trawler, utterly exhausted with two days of hand pumping and dumping coal, the crew manage to clear their pumps and get moving again at half-speed. For economy's sake, the salvage tug is cancelled, and, in quiet anti-climax, the little ship starts to limp back to Aberdeen. Over her patched-up aerial, she thanks the radio station, and everyone looks upon it as a routine winter episode —except that eight men nearly died.

I brought my treatment back to Cavalcanti and we worked out its filmic possibilities. A treatment is really a long short-story, with little dialogue and very few camera instructions. It is terse and factual, with no descriptive elaborations. Writing this way for so long makes it impossible for me to ever attempt to write a novel. For instance, in a novel one might have to say about a sunrise, 'As the first softening light of the morning began to awaken the hidden, sleeping birds, and silhouette the stark trees against . . . etc., etc.', whereas I would write 'Fade-in dawn'. All the rest was up to me, the camera and sound men, when the shooting began.

With a straightforward story-line like this, what we wanted was a good shape and good characterization. We instinctively used the rhetorical shape, that is prologue, thesis, antithesis and synthesis, and I firmly believe that this shape is the ideal one for almost any dramatic story. The emphasis can be varied indefinitely, of course. The prologue can be one establishing shot, or an elaborate sequence. The synthesis can be a tying up of all the loose ends, or the walk away from the camera, the 'reaching-for-your-hat' shot, as we used to call it. But stick to that magic shape and you can't go far wrong.

Characterization comes out in the writing of the shooting script, with its descriptions of the people in the film and their dialogue. I always believed in a very detailed shooting script, with every camera position carefully set down, every action or movement of the cast described, and an indication where each cut would come. In fact, my main imaginative work was done during the writing of this final script, and I was, as it were, seeing it on the screen as I wrote it, because I knew that, because of our poverty and lack of facilities, I would have to improvise madly during the shooting, and I needed a master copy to aim at.

Characterization meant people, and people meant casting. So back I went to Aberdeen to cast my film. I needed a skipper and a mate, two engineers, three deck-hands and a cook, plus their wives and girl-friends, a shipowner, and sundry citizens of Aberdeen. The film was to be three reels, that is half an hour long, and I had £2,000. As usual, it never entered our head to use anybody else but real people, so I went to the Labour Exchange. I sat just behind the official on duty, and listened to the fishermen applying for jobs. I worked on the following rather sad formula. If a chap came up and asked 'Any work?' and then just walked away, no good for me. If, after he was told 'No', he immediately started in with 'Listen, I'm the best deck-hand in the business, I've got all my own gear, and I've just come off the *Loch Buie* and the bo'sun said I was . . ., etc.,' then he was an extrovert, and therefore a potential actor, so into the office for an interview.

My days as an employer recruiting labour at the 'Burroo', as the Scots called the Exchange, were fascinating. A few of the chaps, when I mentioned 'fillums', just laughed at me and pushed off. But most of those I interviewed were immediately interested, even if it was firstly about the money I would pay. I was only offering basic fishermen's rates, which cooled their ardour a good deal, but I also offered a guaranteed three weeks' work, and a bonus. There was no large pool of unemployed in fishing at that moment, so I was seeing the 'roughs', as the officials called them. I was glad. I was looking for faces and personalities, and, by God, I got them. 'A bunch of unemployables' was what one civil servant labelled them when I signed them on, but they were a wonderful gang, and only one let me down. I also decided to augment them with Bill Blewett from Cornwall, which turned out a master-stroke. As a fellow fisherman, he explained the madnesses of film-making to the rest as one who had gone through it and survived, and made acting look so easy that they just strolled through it behind him. (Bill is still alive in Mousehole aged eighty-two, and is as inimitable as ever. When I visited him recently, we foregathered, of course, in the pub. Like Bill, I had on a fisherman's jersey, and as we talked, we must have given every appearance of being a couple of old salts swapping yarns. It was too much for a nosy tourist who kept creeping nearer and nearer. Bill suddenly turned to him and said 'Me and 'Arry 'ere was in the Crimea War together.' You could see the wretched tourist's mind ticking over to try and relate dates. Without a pause Bill went on 'Remember that, 'Arry? You was on the piebald, I had that brown gelding the sergeant-major give me ...' He went on dead-pan, with marvellous outlandish detail for about ten minutes, until the tourist slunk away. That at eighty-two!)

I still hadn't a skipper, the lead player, and utterly vital to the whole story. Skippers didn't deign to go to the 'Burroo' to look for work, so I had to search for my man elsewhere. I soon confirmed what I had found before in casting story documentaries, that the higher you go up the social scale, the worse actors people become. They're so bloody frightened of making fools of themselves, or what the neighbours will say. Shepherds, miners, fishermen, people like that are naturals; bank clerks, accountants, and, as it turned out, trawler skippers, become as stiff as totem-poles in front of a camera.

I tested about a dozen, and, although some of them looked great, they all spoke their lines like a child of ten giving his first recitation at a school concert. I was in despair, when someone mentioned a chap who was away as bo'sun on a long trip on one of the big trawlers. He was colour-blind, so could not get a ticket, but was said to be more intelligent than most skippers, and had done some public speaking for the Union. He was due in at 6 am the next morning, so down I went to the fish quay.

As the big rusty work-worn trawler was docking, I soon spotted a short, compact, gingery man, with about two weeks' growth of beard, supervising the berthing. His voice and manner were sharp and commanding, and in his thick grey jersey and white seaboots, he looked the complete seaman. I shouted down 'Are you Mattie Mair?' He nodded with a 'What the hell does he want?' look in his eye. I plunged straight in 'Would you be interested in playing a skipper in a film about fishing?' What delighted me was that he didn't dither or hesitate. He answered straight away 'I wouldn't mind', so I arranged to meet him at my hotel that evening.

I walked around all day seeing that tough figure playing my

scenes, and waited in the hotel lounge in considerable excitement. I was somewhat irritated, therefore, when a bank manager, in a smart dark suit, dark overcoat, silk scarf, and bowler hat came up and said 'You wanted to see me?' It actually took seconds for me to realize that this was my skipper! I thanked God daily during the making of the film that I'd first seen him at work, because I'd never have been clever enough to choose him otherwise. He gave a magnificent performance, because, while the others just had to be themselves, he had to act. He had to be authoritative, resourceful, optimistic, while frightened inside. He had to slave-drive the crew when they all were dropping with fatigue, yet give them hope and cheer, and he never put a foot wrong.

It was now mid-winter, the right time for the storms we needed, so I sent for my unit, the old faithfuls Jonah Jones and Chick Fowle, and a new assistant, Ralph Elton, brother of one of the originals, Arthur Elton, who had now become the umpteenth baronet. Ralph was a large puppy-clumsy kid, straight from university but eager to learn. He lost us our digs within a week. It was one of those very circumspect Scottish boarding-houses, where a large can of hot water is placed each morning outside your door. Young Elton was always late, so he'd dash out of his room, inevitably fall over the can of water, and let out a stream of oaths. The landlady came to me and said we must go. 'Mr Elton is no gentleman.' It was no good explaining about the rights of sturgeon and swan, or that Elton was, in fact, the only gentleman, by definition, amongst us. Out we went and settled into a seedy hotel—at winter rates.

I had chartered one of the oldest trawlers in the harbour, the *John Gillman*, which was actually waiting to go to the ship-breakers, so was cheap. My ragged-arsed crew manned her and prepared her for sea. There was no question of a working crew and an acting crew—it never entered our head. They would have to do both, and to make some money, we even decided to fish as well!

Waiting for the storms that we knew would soon come, we got on with the opening sequences. We were showing the various members of the crew making their way through the deserted early morning streets to join their ship for another routine voyage. As sometimes happens in Scotland in winter, we got some lovely cold sunny days, with an incredibly clear thin light. In it, the dour old city looked beautiful, with the bleak outlines of the terraced cottages softened by the smoke of the newly-lit fires. Everything was going fine, when we got an astonishing hold-up. I had cast a woman of about thirty-five as the skipper's wife. All she had to do was say 'Cheerio then, see you Saturday' at the cottage door, and she looked exactly right. The day we came to shoot this scene, it had snowed, so we spent half the day clearing it off the whole cottage, roof and all. Then I sent Elton for the wife. He came back and said 'She won't come'. I did one of my jumping-up-and-down-and-cursing-while-tearing-my-hair acts, went off to get her, and found myself involved in a rather moving little scene. This woman was the last of a family that had married and moved away, and she was left behind looking after her father. Nothing had ever happened in her life until suddenly she was casually offered this tiny scene in a real film. It was romance, it was colour, at last. And on the very day it all was to occur her father came back from the sea, and he was Salvation Army! He had laid it right on the line—if she appeared in this sinful exhibition of lewdness and lechery, she could get out. The woman was in tears when I got to their house, but still wanted to play the part, so I started to explain what kind of film it was, but suddenly gave up. I could see that this dreadful piece of self-righteous granite meant what he said, and I would have split-up their pathetic association if I had succeeded. In fact, it was a good thing the old bigot returned when he did. If his daughter had appeared in the film, she might well have been cast out— literally—into the snow.

Then the storms came, and we put to sea. As the other boats were scurrying for shelter, the *John Gillman* chugged out, to lots of derisory remarks and forecasts of doom from the dockside loungers, to portray a ship in distress.

We sought out the least sheltered spots, the tide-races, where the seas were roughest, and found, to our consternation, that the fine old craft was so well-designed and seaworthy that she rode everything like a duck. I wanted the decks awash, and they were almost dry. So back we came to harbour, and crippled the gallant vessel by stowing sixty barrels of water in her bows. By God, she shipped them then!

The next three weeks was a kaleidoscope of smashing seas, screaming wind, cold—always cold—and the utter fatigue of just trying to keep upright and dry, while doing a job. Real seas are very difficult to photograph—realistically. Any holiday-maker who has snapped the apparently big waves from a steamer will realize how the camera flattens them out. The *John Gillman*, therefore, had to sail at the angles where she shipped most water or roll her scuppers under, or plunge at full speed at the biggest seas, while the film crew set up the camera, and I endeavoured to put some of the cast through a scene. And often there would be a yell of 'Look out!' from the skipper in the wheelhouse, everyone would dash to hang on, and a great cold rushing sea would cover us. The camera would be soaked, so the boys had to go below, take it to bits, and dry it out. One hour, two hours later, we would try the same scene again, with often the same result. It was the most fearful, tiring, frustrating, yet exciting episode I ever shot. We got only a few seconds of the film each day, and we didn't fake a foot.

The routine was that we left harbour at 6 am, to get out of the shelter of the land by the time there was enough light to shoot. We generally got back around eight at night, after which the cameras had to be cleaned, the magazines refilled, exposed film packed and dispatched to London, and the previous day's rushes viewed, which didn't leave much time for night-clubbing, if Aberdeen had boasted a night club. In reasonable weather, we tried staying out all night and fishing, but it was so crowded on board and the catch so poor, it wasn't worth it. We did sell about thirty quid's worth of fish, and I often wondered under what heading the Post Office put that item.

The one member of the cast that let me down was the cook. He had been the only cook applying for work when I was cast-ing, so I was more or less stuck with him. Apart from being a dreadful cook, he was a drunk. One morning he failed to turn up at the 6 am rendezvous. We waited two hours, and he eventually appeared, still pissed. I gave him a broadside of well-chosen adjectives and he answered me back in kind. So I lost my temper and said, somewhat melodramatically 'Put that man ashore!' I had forgotten what authority I had, as titular owner of the ship. Before I could change my mind, two of the crew seized the wretched cook and slung him onto the quay. Another chucked his poor belongings after him, and, in a moment, that pasty-faced, wobbly figure, standing there alone on the wet grey cobblestones, took on an infinite pathos. I suddenly, desperately wanted to call him back, but Mattie Mair's shout of 'Let go for'ard' stopped me. That frightening moment of complete power has always stayed with me.

We decided to do the interiors in our studio in London, and this brought considerable problems. I've mentioned it was about the size of a village hall, and a replica of the cabins of the *John Gillman*, which consisted of the main feeding-sleeping quarters, plus an adjacent captain's cubby-hole, doubling as the radio room, almost filled it. After that we had to get our lights and cameras into position. The real poser was that this set had to rock—not only rock, but heave and roll and jolt to match up with the gyrations of the *John Gillman* at sea. Ingenuity and improvisation were the watchwords of prewar documentary, and a young stillsman, Jack Bryson, working with our only carpenter, came up with a brilliant solution. They constructed a deep saucer of heavy timbers, and built the set on top of this. Jutting out from the saucer were four battens, at north, south, east and west, as it were. All we had to do was put a bloke on each batten, and they could roll or jerk the set at will. The camera was placed on a raised platform level with the set, and never needed to be moved. The set was just twisted round to it, and we thus could get superb angles. Say I wanted to shoot into the main cabin past a figure sleeping in a bunk, the saucer would be spun around until the bunk was in front of the camera, the backing panel removed, and there was the sleeping man in front of you. I could then, looking through the camera, have the set moved inches either way until the angle was perfect. It was as simple and foolproof a method of shooting on a moving set as I have ever seen, and yet no art director I told about it later would ever try it.

The trip to London was a big adventure for the crew who had never been away from Scotland, and they fell right into the fake of studio shooting. As a famous Scots comedian used to say 'it was nae bother a'taw'. The set looked so realistic—as they had brought their fishing clothes with them, it soon smelled realistic too—that they just continued being themselves, and Mattie Mair, by now a highly accomplished actor, was superb.

Cavalcanti, who had been, of course, advising, criticizing, and helping me throughout all this, had also been supervising the editing, and we got the film out fairly soon after the interiors were finished. It got marvellous notices, and went out on the cinema circuits! We had succeeded in our belief that documentary could compete with 'synthetic' films, and that people would gladly pay to see them. In Scotland, the film was a smash hit, and it apparently popped up in Aberdeen as regularly as the Xmas Pantomime. The most extraordinary story about it is what I learnt only recently, when I asked the Central Office of Information to show me the film again to refresh my memory. They told me that it is still being booked, after thirty-two years! So I suppose that torment on the *John Gillman* was worth it.

*　　*　　*　　*　　*

Another result of the success of *North Sea* was that the commercial cinema stopped sneering at us, and started offering me jobs. I was asked to go down to Denham, where they were preparing to make the original version of *Goodbye Mr Chips*, with Robert Donat. I saw some American big-shot, who as usual, started off by saying 'I saw your little picture, and I must tell you I liked it'. This patronizing attitude, though meant well, always irritated me, because a film like *North Sea*, done on the spot, with practically no technical facilities and amateur actors, was a bloody sight harder to make than most features. However, he had a big desk and a big cigar, so I let it pass. He then offered me the job of directing the second unit of *Mr Chips*, and added something that delighted me. He said, 'Your trouble is that you have no experience of shooting in a studio'. I then happily told him that all the interiors of *North Sea* had been done in the studio, and he wouldn't believe me! This guy was a so-called tycoon, and our quiet little stillsman and our one carpenter had baffled his Hollywood expertise! He was also a bore, so I did not take the job.

I did, however, take a second unit job on a big spectacular called *Jamaica Inn*, because it was being directed by Alfred Hitchcock, the only British feature director we respected. I wasn't whoring after the big time. We looked upon it rather as slumming for a while to earn a bit of extra scratch, and maybe pick up some new tips, but there was never any idea of making it permanent, or deserting documentary for long.

From my point of view the whole episode was a bit of a flop. As is typical of this crazy business, I had been basically engaged to direct a storm scene in a tank, because I had filmed one at sea! I had never even seen a tank, and it was really a job for highly-trained special-effects people. Before doing the tank stuff, I found that a second unit job was just picking up detail shots left behind by the main unit—things like galloping horses' hooves or doubles falling out of windows, and so on. To my regret, I didn't get to work with Hitchcock at all. I did watch him when I could, and he was a tremendously skilled film-maker. As he had originally been an art director, he could draw the shots he wanted, and one day he gave me a lesson, with drawings, on the use of camera angles, which I never forgot. What it came down to was always use a camera angle to help tell the story, never just tilt your camera because you think it looks cute, or you want to seem clever. At its simplest, if you want a man to appear small and insignificant, you shoot down on him, if you want him to look strong and menacing, you shoot up. A car, rushing at you, is twice as frightening from a low angle. But all these unusual angles are precious, to be used only at the right moment to get the maximum effect. If they are used in the wrong place, they just look pretentious and gimmicky, like so many present-day films.

Hitch was jovial and amusing on the floor, but a lot of his humour had an undercurrent of the sadism that shows up in his films. We had on the unit a young, very camp, period expert— the film story was set around the early 1800s. He knew his stuff all right, and would blow his top if he found, say an 1830 salt-cellar in an 1815 banqueting scene. One day, Hitch had horses on the set and, just as they were starting to shoot, one of them did an enormous pile right in front of the camera. Hitch stopped everything, and sent for the period expert to come, urgently. He rushed panting onto the set with 'Yes, Mr Hitchcock?' Pointing dramatically to the huge turd, Hitch said 'Is that in period?' It got an enormous laugh at the time, but, in front of a hundred people, it was pretty cruel.

The cast was, as they say, star-studded, headed by Charles Laughton, and including the young Maureen O'Hara, in her first film, apart from one easily forgotten B-picture. At nineteen, she was absolutely beautiful, and, as an actress, absolutely clueless. I was suddenly asked by Erich Pommer, the ex-Czar of all the German studios, who was producing the film, and who, incidentally was, to me, by far the most interesting person connected with it, to pick up a shot with Maureen that had been missed by the main unit. It was a simple little job. The story was the Daphne du Maurier one about Cornish wreckers and a wicked squire, and young Bob Newton—later, alas, to become one of the monumental drunks of the business—was the juvenile, and Maureen's boy-friend. They had already shot a scene where Bob was being strung up by the neck by the wreckers. The shot I had to do was where Maureen peers through a tiny crack in the wall of an attic, sees what is happening, reacts, and then dashes off for help.

When I got on the set it all seemed easy. Nice set, good bunch of boys, pretty young actress. I do remember being irritated because she kept eating buttered toast, which dribbled and spoilt her make-up, but, what the hell, it was only one shot. I showed Maureen the hole in the wall, checked she knew the scene and what was supposed to be happening next door, and tried a rehearsal. She ambled up to the crack, stuck a huge violet eye against it, uttered the sort of squeak a girl makes when she's been goosed at a party, and disappeared from the frame in the wrong direction. I wasn't too discouraged. I had spent years handling amateurs, so I gave her a little chat, and tried again. It was worse! Now it was up to me to show what I could do. I gave her the works—that the man there next door, hanging by his neck, was the man whose touch she thrilled to, whose kisses she adored and longed for, in whose arms she would lie naked, who would father her children, AND HE WAS CHOKING TO DEATH! I even did a choking act. 'Right, in you go, kid, and remember, take a moment to realize the whole horror of it. Then, your eyes open wide, you hold the look for, say, two seconds, then you turn your head slowly towards camera, remember, towards camera, as though you are hardly able to grasp what is going on in the next room, and then try and let us see your sudden decision to rush off and get help.

But *don't* move fast until you have made that decision. Do you understand that now?' Maureen understood perfectly, moved up to the hole, and gave an impression of someone watching 'What The Butler Saw'. She got the giggles! It was my choking act, she said. I think the camera crew watched carefully to step in before I did it to her.

I filmed that one goddam shot all afternoon—twenty odd takes, and then rushed off to Pommer: 'Mr Pommer,' I said 'I'm sorry, I just can't get a performance out of that O'Hara kid. I know why, mind you, she's a virgin, and until someone gives her a good roll, she's got about as much animation as a piece of wet cod. But I'm afraid I've let you down.' Pommer, chewing nervously on an empty cigarette holder, as he always did, agreed with me, but speaking from his experience, cheered me up by saying she was so lovely that people would not worry about her performance.

At the end of the picture, it was discovered that she had been secretly married to an assistant director all the time. So much for my sixth-sense about actors.

There was a most unholy row when Maureen's marriage became known. The Laughton-Pommer Company, Mayflower Productions, was proposing to go and make films in Hollywood, and one of their major assets was their dewy unspoilt Irish rose, who would no doubt be excellent bait for the financial tycoons. The whole matter was hushed up, and Maureen was shipped off to the States with assurances, I believe, to the boy that he would follow. But time went on, and by now immersed in the process of being groomed as a star, Maureen agreed to a discreet divorce to be arranged. I don't think they ever saw each other again.

5

I returned happily to documentaries, with some cash in the bank for the birth of our first child, a considerable respect for the technical skill of feature film-makers but with, at the same time, a contempt for the luxury and waste that seemed to be accepted as part of the circus. I also brought the first reverse recruit to documentary with me, a bright young chap called Julian Spiro, who eagerly agreed to swop seven quid a week knocking on star's dressing-room doors for three quid and a chance to create. He was to make some fine war films.

I straight away made another obligatory picture, this time on the work of the Accountant-General's Department called *Big Money*, which was a hard one to make anything of, but gave me some fascinating insights into the behind-the-scenes workings of Government finance, and a new appreciation of the much maligned civil servants. But war was on the way, and we began to get hints of our probable involvement.

We were asked, early in 1939, in a roundabout and tentative manner, if we could make, under strict security, an animated diagram film, to be used to teach certain unspecified scientific developments. We know now it was radar, but as no-one would tell us anything specific, and we did not have a clue what was wanted, we soon got bogged down in a typical official impasse. We finally explained that we had no facilities to make cartoon or animated films, but could set up a complete department in about six weeks, at considerable cost. We never heard anything more, and I don't know if that vital film was ever made. What had been established by that approach, however, was that we were going to be the official war film unit.

Despite the clouds of war, propaganda was still a dirty word in Britain, and advertising was considered vulgar. Propaganda was what those tiresome foreigners went in for, and we did not need to advertise our obvious virtues. So, while desperate efforts were being made elsewhere to catch up with the lethargy and neglect of the thirties, practically nothing was done to plan or prepare for the dissemination of official information, or analyse the vast public relations network that would be needed. In fact, the Ministry of Information was not even formed until after war broke out.

Somebody must have been thinking ahead, however, because we were instructed to lay in large stores of film stock, and authorized to buy some new equipment, mostly cameras. Then, about ten days before the actual declaration of war, we were ordered to make a short instructional film, based on an official handbook, called *If War Should Come*. This was just a straightforward statement of what the public should do when the air raid sirens sounded.

We rushed off to outlandish parts of London, collected friends and acquaintances—it was supposed to be secret—and made them walk 'in an orderly manner' into the air raid shelters, 'check their gas masks', and 'obey the air raid wardens at all times'. Strung together, it was factual and somehow phoney. We then got an order to have thousands of copies printed, and organize a nationwide distribution of the film when we were given the word. We had to hand the main job over to professional distributors, of course, but we filled up all our own transport with copies, mapped out the cinemas of London, and waited. The fatal Sunday of 3 September 1939 came, and immediately after Chamberlain's speech, saying war had been declared, the sirens went off. To this day, no-one seems to know with certainty whether it was a genuine warning or a mistake. What was certain was that nobody behaved the way they were supposed to in our film. Everybody just went into the streets and gawped at the sky, delighted in the balloons, laughed at the air raid wardens, and chatted with each other in the new-found camaraderie that—alas—makes people so nostalgic about wars. The authorities obviously thought again, our little film was canned, and the thousands of copies presumably scrapped.

Next day we got orders to get out of our familiar headquarters in Soho Square and move to the offices of a publicity film company called Spectator Films, in Savile Row.

Apparently our premises, old and cosy as they were, might be vulnerable, while the Savile Row place was brand new and concrete. Working at full pressure, within a week we were ready in the new headquarters, poised for action, with half a dozen fully equipped units, miles of film, enormous enthusiasm —and, of course, nothing happened at all! Nothing, not even waffling words of encouragement, or meaningless memos. It was only later that we discovered the abyss of chaos that was our new administrators, the Ministry of Information. Because his section of the Post Office had included us, a pompous Scot called Highet had been made head of the films division. This meant that the whole film effort of Britain at war, both instructional and propaganda, was controlled by someone whose total creative problems had been bounded by whether to paint the Post Office at Nether Wallop white or pink!

Of course, some very fine brains had been recruited into the lower echelons of the film division, including John Betjeman, whose lovely sense of fun helped us to survive those exasperating early days. He had been given a minuscule office, which he immediately carpeted, and equipped with a rather good desk from his own home. This, of course, under Civil Service rules, classified him as a senior official. Regulars, bursting in on him, stopped in their tracks, and wondered if they should call him 'Sir'. So impressed were they that someone decided his room should be repainted and two representatives of the Office of Works, in white overalls, duly arrived to carry this out. Part of a painter's uniform in those days was plimsolls, so our two blokes removed their boots, packed them neatly by Betjeman's desk, and started sloshing on the paint. John stood it for a while, and then wrote a memo to the Director-General, something like this: (1) I have been recruited to this department to do important war work (2) I have of necessity to concentrate on the propaganda value of every word I write (3) I find this creative process very difficult while two worthy gentlemen splash whitewash around my office. (Signed) John Betjeman. P.S. My office also smells of feet!

John, the perennial schoolboy, also joyfully joined us in our campaign to get rid of Highet. His method was somewhat bizarre. When he heard Highet get in the lift, he would dart out of his office and proclaim, in an appalling imitation of a

Scottish accent, 'Highet, yourr dooom is sealed!' It is doubtful if this broke Highet's nerve, but he did disappear. Alas, this was much later.

Back at Savile Row, we were going mad. As all the work in progress had been cancelled on the declaration of war, we had absolutely nothing to do at all. We began to pass the time by watching the tarts in the street below, and soon got so fascinated by their turnover, if that is the word, that we started running a book on their activities. You could bet on how many clients a girl would get in a set period, or whether the next one would be a soldier or a civvy, or how quickly she'd be back on the beat after an assignation—this figure was astonishing. Some of the keener betting men in the unit inspected the field at close quarters, and the girls soon got names like Mouldy Maisie, Skinny Lizzie, or The Duchess, who hid her pathetic raddled face under picture hats. This was horrible and wasteful, of course, and we made one more plea to the Ministry for a directive—and got nothing.

It was then that Cavalcanti, magnificent old Cav, the alien, whom some Blimps always suspected, took the law into his own hands, and sent us all into the streets to film anything we saw that was new and different. Cav realized that history was being made all around us, and a tremendous opportunity to record it for posterity was being lost, so six small units went out with all our film stock and filmed the extraordinary scenes of a nation amateurishly preparing its capital for a new kind of war. We filmed the frantic sandbag filling, the new balloons rising up in the oddest places, the endless drilling in the parks, the new auxiliary policemen—I remember I got a chap in plus-fours and monocle directing traffic at Piccadilly Circus—anything that was different from the normal peacetime way of life.

By the end of about ten days, we had an enormous amount of material and still no word from the Ministry, so, absolutely off our own bat, we decided to make a film of it. Too late, we realized that, in our panic to do something, we should have shot to a plan rather than off the cuff, but we bashed out a script, and, with the help of an excellent commentary by Robert Sinclair, produced a half-hour picture we called *The First Days*. We weren't very happy about it, thinking of it as a rather disjointed record of the obvious, but seen today it is extraordinarily moving, with one sequence, of the farewells of the troops leaving for France, over which the commentator repeats 'Goodbye', quietly and almost casually, is still tear-jerking. It is also now, of course, a classic for the archives, as Cavalcanti foresaw.

Off we went to the Ministry and proudly announced 'We've made a film', and they really replied 'Good God!' They seemed genuinely shocked that someone had actually done something, and horrified when we asked them to handle it for us. Apparently, a committee was going to be formed to discuss whether Government films should be given away free or distributed normally through the trade. And now these awkward blighters had made one—most inconsiderate! As it would obviously take weeks for them to decide their policy, they hedged their responsibility by telling us—unofficially, of course—to do what we liked with the film. So Cavalcanti and I, with the three tins under our arm, hawked the first British official movie up and down Wardour Street, like a couple of hard-up independent producers! We didn't get much enthusiasm, but eventually Pathé, shrewd enough to see that there would be many more Government films, agreed to distribute it—and pay for it, which was still important to us. I have always believed that that contract persuaded the Government to sell their films rather than give them away, which, over the war years, must have brought in an enormous sum.

We were suddenly ordered back to Soho Square. No reason was given, but it is interesting that Savile Row was badly bombed and Soho Square never got a scratch. We were starting to rot again when in walked our saviour in the shape of an Air Vice-Marshal Boyd, the commanding officer of the Balloon Barrage. He went straight to the point. 'I understand you are the official Government film unit, will you make me a film?' We chorused 'Yes sir, please sir', and asked for the story. Apparently, morale in Balloon Command was at a very low ebb. The men now manning the balloons had been Territorials, local shopkeepers, bank managers, representatives and the like, who had enjoyed swanking around in Air Force uniform in peacetime, but who actively detested tending a recalcitrant balloon from a tent on the mudflats around Liverpool or the mouth of the Thames, particularly as there seemed to be no danger or even no war. A lot of the lads had simply packed it in and gone home. The Air Vice-Marshal wanted us to make a morale-boosting film, to show the value and necessity of the balloon barrage and why the continual vigilance of all concerned was vital. Boyd was way ahead of his contemporaries, because it was at least a year later before the Services got even an inkling of the value of propaganda.

I was given the job, and pretty soon found myself stuck for ideas. As soon as I went out around the balloon sites, I understood why the troops were so fed-up. It was a ghastly job. Balloons were boring things to start with, lunging around at the end of their cables like elephants that have had bad news, liable to break away in the middle of the night and have to be chased across the countryside, and the sites themselves were often in the dreariest and most inaccessible places. They were never meant to stop bombing but to prevent the Germans diving on the target, their terrifying new technique, and force them to bomb from a height, a very inaccurate method in those days. I couldn't think of an angle by which I could make them at all interesting or attractive until suddenly the Germans saved my bacon. They put on a small bomber raid on the warships around the Forth Bridge, and, believe it or not, there wasn't a balloon within a hundred miles! They were all concentrated round the dock areas, and immediately there was a frantic rush to move them to the naval bases, including the Forth area. Here was my theme, and I was off.

I told the story of one squadron, through the training and preparation, to the day of the Forth Bridge raid when they get orders to pack up and move from Cardington, in Bedfordshire, to Scotland in twenty-four hours. A squadron, with all the winch lorries, ancillary transport, repair shops, stores and so on, had over fifty vehicles and two hundred men, so it was a big job. We shot the preliminaries in appalling weather, but the strange gloom gave an unexpectedly dramatic effect, particularly to the scenes of the long convoy snaking across the flat Bedfordshire countryside. Then we set off for Scotland, to reconstruct the whole German raid! I was as usual over-ambitious, because one must remember that there was no war-time library material to draw upon, and everything had to be reconstructed from scratch. I really don't think we would have succeeded if we hadn't, right at the beginning, become involved in a ridiculous, typically British balls-up.

The German raid had been a complete failure, and several of their slow two-engined bombers had been shot down by our Hurricanes and Spitfires, including one into the sea, the crew of which was picked up by a small fishing boat. I got hold of some old bits of a plane, painted Swastikas on them, hired three hearties from Edinburgh University to impersonate the Jerries, and planned to reconstruct this episode, using the actual fishing boat. The day we were to shoot this was beautifully sunny, but blowing half a gale, far too rough to put the 'varsity boys, now dressed in German Luftwaffe uniforms, into the sea. I asked the fishermen where we could find some calmer waters, and they replied 'Back of the island' pointing out to Inchkeith, a large island in the middle of the Firth of Forth. So off we set, getting well soaked on the way. We soon found a sheltered bay, launched the bits of plane and the phoney Jerries, and started to film. Then a high-speed launch dashed at us, and we were under arrest by the Navy!

A delighted sub-lieutenant, very self-important in his first command, escorted us into the little harbour, and with a lot of saluting and countersigning, we were formally handed over to the Army. The three 'varsity boys and the fishermen were left on board their boat, but the film crew, that is myself, Jonah Jones and my new assistant, Julian Spiro, the refugee from commercialism, were marched off under armed guard, searched and chucked into the detention cell! Nobody would listen to our protests and explanations—we were obviously spies. They took away our camera gear, not realizing we had swopped film magazines on the way in, an old newsreelman's trick, but they unexpectedly left a bottle of whisky, which I had prudently invested in before venturing on the briny. So Julian and I proceeded to get pleasantly sloshed—Jonah didn't drink—while debating our fate. It was obvious that we had landed ourselves in some very hush-hush area, but we were Government employees, with Ministry of Information passes, so were convinced that once the CO of the island made a telephone call, he'd be down, full of apologies, and might even ask us to lunch. We stayed in the cell all day! Our only visitors were local civilians, who had heard of the Jerry spies, and who periodically shouted through the barred window 'I hope they shoot you'. We demonstrated the thoroughness of the Germans' training of their agents in the vernacular by answering amicably, 'Go and get stuffed'.

Long after dark, we were suddenly hustled out of the hut, handed over to the Navy again, with a lot more saluting and signing, and put aboard an armed trawler, which set off for Leith. There a Black Maria was waiting for us, and several enormous policemen escorted us to the Central Police Station. By this time, the euphoria of the whisky had worn off, and I was getting very angry. I demanded to see a top man, and asked him why he hadn't telephoned the Ministry in London and checked our credentials. He blandly replied that he had done so, and nobody knew anything about us! Then the penny dropped. It was Saturday afternoon and, for our war-weary bosses, that meant a little tidying in the garden or a round of golf. The one duty-officer didn't even know there was a film section. Then the police grilled us, and when I see the mamby-pamby stuff in *Dixon of Dock Green* I sometimes think of those huge Highlanders whose hard blue eyes seemed to bore through you. Although you knew you were innocent, they somehow made you feel guilty. Suddenly about two in the morning we were released. Presumably someone had actually vouched for us.

We woke up next day to find ourselves a great joke in all the Scottish papers. What had happened was that an enterprising journalist had heard about the missing fishing boat, and eventually got the whole story in time for the Sundays. Wherever we went after that we were welcomed as the 'German Spies', and the publicity helped more than all the permits or passes in getting us cooperation.

I discovered an excellent description of the raid in a BBC radio programme, in which they interviewed all the eye-witnesses they could find, and determined to follow it completely factually. The Air Force, elated with their first aerial victory, helped marvellously and did a thing for me that I suppose was unique in the whole of that wartime—they actually painted Swastikas on Blenheims, two-engined planes very similar in outline to the ones the Germans used, and recreated the actual raid. Then the fighters got in amongst them, and we got some of the best aerial combat stuff of the war. I said some time back that it was in this film, which we called *Squadron 992*, that I had a sequence that I would show again. Because I am still proud of it, I'd like to try and describe it. Two of the eye-witnesses involved in the original raid were miners out on the moors with a whippet for a pleasant day's poaching. They were about to release the dog after a hare when an aerial battle started right over their heads, and, with bullets flying everywhere, they dived for a ditch. I took this episode and enlarged it. I set the camera up on a small hill in open moorland and got a fighter and a phoney bomber to chase around us, as close as possible. Then from the same set-up, I set a whippet chasing a hare and cross-cut the dog and the hare with the fighter and the bomber, but counter-pointed the sound. Once, we actually got all four of them in one shot! Then at the moment the dog caught the hare, I put over it the tremendous bang of the bomber crashing. The whole sequence only lasts about two minutes, but it makes the film cinematically worthwhile.

We did the small amount of interior scenes in our studio, and brought a bunch of airmen up from Cardington to appear in them. On the lorry they sang a song new to me, 'Bless 'Em All', but they were using that over-worked four-letter word instead of 'Bless'. Walter Leigh, a young musician whom I think would have become one of Britain's top composers if he had not been tragically killed in action, was to do the music, and I got the boys to sing their song for him. We both liked it so much that he made it the theme for the film, and we even got out a clean version to be sung on the long trek north. Being eager young simpletons, only wanting to do our bit, we forgot one vital thing—to copyright it. After the first showing of the film, Tin Pan Alley spotted the song, and grabbed it. I suppose it must have been used in every film or television programme made about the war ever since, and if we had not been so naïve, Walter Leigh's family would have had a nice steady income for life. It is sad that the brilliant rearrange-ments and ingenious orchestrations he made of the tune now sound hackneyed, because of the way it has been over-plugged and over-used.

Squadron 992 was also a war casualty. Just after it had its first showing, the war had started in earnest, and it was out of date. Apart from a facetious and truncated version shown in America called *Flying Elephants*, it never saw the light of day.

There was also a sad sequel for the enterprising Air Vice-Marshal Boyd. Promoted to be Air Officer Commanding, Middle East, in November 1940, his plane force landed in Sicily, and he was in the bag until 1943, when he escaped, only to die of his privations in 1944.

The Ministry of Information had, at last, sorted itself out. The Films Division was taken over by Sidney Bernstein, of Granada Cinemas, and Jack Beddington, head of Shell Publicity, both highly professional and dedicated men. We became the Crown Film Unit, and were to work non stop for the next two years. While all the other members of the Unit were started on various projects, I was sent down to Dover with Jonah Jones, to cover everything we found interesting or exciting, and try and make a film out of it. We arrived just in time to meet the remnants of the British Army returning from Dunkirk. We immediately applied to go over and film the evacuation, but were refused, with the argument that the space we two would occupy might mean the lives of two soldiers. It was a hard one to answer, but I will regret, to my dying day, that I didn't fiddle it somehow. The Germans made enormous propaganda out of their films of the British prisoners and the chaos of the beaches. If we could have shown the discipline of the Guards, or the incredible cheeriness of everyone in defeat, we could have had a morale-boosting film that would have shaken the world. As it was, we just shot the troops landing at Dover, sad, weaponless and beaten.

We stayed at the Grand Hotel, the only one left standing, and our fellow guests made it fascinating, because they were all journalists, including many Americans. These were the vultures and jackals of the war, who admitted they were there to report on the fall of Britain. They had been on the spot to see all Europe conquered, so now they had their new headlines ready. And don't let us kid ourselves; many of them, at that time, were not our gallant allies. Quite a lot were contemptuous of our pathetic defiance, and were much more impressed with the might they had seen rising up across the Channel.

When I was taken round our local defences, I could understand the Americans' outspoken opinion that we hadn't a hope. I knew nothing of war, but the succession of 1914–18 weapons, block-houses that obviously could not have withstood one shell, and the naïve belief that barbed wire and indiscriminate lumps of concrete could contain Panzer tanks, made even me realize that, for the loss of a few thousand men, the Germans could walk it. The Regular Army people I came across didn't give me much more confidence either, brave as they no doubt were, I was generally met by some chinless wonder of a subaltern, who would say with an asinine guffaw 'You're one of those chaps who wear their cap round the wrong way, and wind a handle, eh?' (His father must have told him about D. W. Griffith.) Then he'd go on 'Well, just pop round to the sergeants' mess, will you, and I'll have a word with the Adjutant'. By the end of the war they were asking would we like a raid put on for the cameras!

I decided to concentrate on the town of Dover, and how it was coping with everything that was happening to it and around it—and that was plenty. The Battle of Britain was at its height, and the dogfights whirled above us constantly, surprisingly similar to what I had faked in Scotland. This led to the daily balloon bashing. The Luftwaffe fighter pilots, mad young kids like our own chaps, used to return to base, after escorting their bombers, in a long shallow dive, scream over Dover at maximum knots, and try and shoot down a balloon or two on the way. Everyone, but everyone, waited for this, not to run for cover, but to have a go at the Jerries. Cooks, batmen, orderlies, signalmen, all the people most unlikely to fire a rifle in anger, were determined to show their prowess. As a result, as soon as the first fighter appeared, an incredible fusillade broke out from the most unexpected places, and it became much more dangerous on the ground than in the air, for I never saw a German plane even quiver. These balloon attacks became so common that another very British phenomenon arose. A betting ring was started on how many balloons would be shot down each day. I remember cowering beside the hotel with the Americans during a real attack on the balloons, when hell was zipping all around us, and seeing an airman, standing completely in the open, yelling at the Jerries to shoot down *his* balloon, because he'd bet against it! This shook the Americans, and may have left a tiny belief in their minds that, while quite mad, we might have something.

Jonah and I had one memorable day. We started by filming, from the beach, a British convoy being shelled from the other side. As I have explained, we were using Newman-Sinclair cameras, with only two minutes shooting time to each magazine, which necessitated constant reloading. This was done in a changing bag, a black cloth contraption into which you inserted the exposed magazine, a new tin of film, an empty tin, and by a masterly piece of legerdemain, you emptied the magazine, transferred the exposed film to the empty tin, and then refilled the magazine from the full tin. Easy when you knew how, but not so easy under fire. I had just taken over the camera, and Jonah had immersed himself in the changing bag, when the Germans lost the range, and a shell hit the water about fifty yards in front of us. Through the camera it looked about ten feet away, so I fell over backwards, to see Jonah, transfixed within his black tent, unable to move, but still determined not to expose his precious film. We stayed like that, petrified, for about twenty seconds, waiting for the next one, which luckily never came. We had hardly pulled ourselves together, when I heard the never-to-be-forgotten sound of a plane crashing. We were, by now, used to the sound of fighters diving in combat, but when the roaring whine suddenly became higher and higher, until it rose to a scream of terrible anguish, then you knew someone had bought it. High in the sky above us a dot was getting bigger and bigger, and Jonah, the perfect cameraman, swung his long-focus lens onto it. The plane crashed into the sea about 200 yards in front of us, bounced, and then disappeared in a tremendous spout of water and we filmed it all. We were already becoming so attuned to the cynicism of war that our first reaction was only that we had got a wonderful end for our film! (This is another shot that appears regularly in war films. I have seen it used as a German, British, American and Russian plane.)

By that time we had about everything in the can, except an actual airman, preferably a German, coming down by

parachute, and, damme, if it didn't happen that very afternoon. We heard this dogfight, and then there was a parachute
at about 20,000 feet, so we piled into our car and started to
chase it. It was drifting fairly fast as it came down, and we
soon found ourselves well out in the country. The lanes
obviously didn't always run the way we wanted to go, so
eventually we had to abandon the car, and start running. A
camera and half a dozen magazines weigh a lot, and that
bloody parachute seemed suddenly to stop descending and
just drift sideways. We ran and ran, over fields, through hedges,
into ditches, until at last the parachute landed, and we caught
up with it. It was a young German, shot through the bottom,
but not badly. He lay and groaned, and we were so buggered
we just lay down beside him. It must have astonished the
country bobby who eventually turned up on a bicycle to find
three bodies instead of one.

He dealt very gently with the wounded pilot while we
hauled ourselves wearily to our feet and set up the camera.
When the young German saw this, he immediately tried to
hide his face and shouted 'Nicht fotografen'. The motherly
old copper turned to us and, to our astonishment, said 'No
photographing!' We smartly answered 'Whose bloody side are
you on?' and took the shot, but it didn't mean much now the
man was on the ground.

$$* \quad * \quad * \quad * \quad *$$

The film, called *Dover—Front Line*, was finished in a hurry, as
they all had to be in those days, and I took it along to show
to my new bosses at the Ministry, Bernstein and Beddington.
They seemed to like it, but then started whispering together
and suddenly turned to me and asked me if I would care to
work with Movietone News. We felt pretty superior to the
newsreels, so I replied 'Not a lot.' They explained that they
had commissioned a ten-minute film for America on London
in the blitz—which by now was at its height—to be made from
newsreel material, and thought I could advise on it. I reluctantly agreed to go along and look at the material, and what
I saw horrified me. A newsreel cameraman is trained to get
maximum impact from his shots, which must tell their story
in a minute or so, without any build-up. Thus, in an air crash

or an earthquake, master-shots, showing as much chaos or devastation as possible are his principal aim, with perhaps a few details to be used as cut-ins and link shots, added afterwards. When sent out to film the results of the blitz, he continued to shoot in this way, and the more devastation he could show, the better the newsreel shot. This wasn't the cameraman's fault. He wasn't making propaganda, but just showing the facts the best way he could. But the two hours of film I saw would have convinced anyone that the whole of London was completely flattened.

I rushed back to the Ministry and suggested the Crown Film Unit should make the film. Bernstein and Beddington were sympathetic but there were a lot of snags. The contract, at a pound a foot, had been given to Movietone, and the film was already booked in America, and must be completely finished in a fortnight. I guaranteed the delivery date, and asked if I could try and sort out the contract problem. With the Ministry's blessing, I went back and saw Sir Gordon Craig, head of Movietone, and suggested we edited the film, with a guarantee we would pay him a pound a foot for all material we got from him. This no doubt sounded like a good deal to him: he would have no editing, no recording of commentary or music, no re-recording or negative cutting to do, and he would get the same price per foot. Of course, I led him to believe that we would get all the material for the film from his firm, which I had not the slightest intention of doing. He gladly waived his contract. In the end I'm afraid we bought seven feet of film from him!

Having fiddled the green light, I hurried back to Soho Square, and we called a general meeting. Humphrey Jennings and I had already discussed the angle we should take on a film about the blitz, so all we had now to do was drop everything and organize everyone to try and meet the almost impossible dateline. I bashed out a two-page treatment on the theme that 'London Carries On'. That, every morning, no matter how hard she is hit, she gets up off the floor like a really tough boxer, and fights back. Then our six little units went out again, and I don't suppose, in the next ten days, we had more than three hours' sleep a night. I was to liaise with the Ministries during the day and shoot the interiors and some blitz stuff at night, while Humphrey coordinated the exterior units, both night and day. McAllister was to edit.

During this hectic time, everyone had narrow squeaks, because we naturally went where the action was thickest, and, contrary to general belief nowadays, we seldom went into air raid shelters, unless to film. One of our favourite places for a quick kip was a large flat Ralph Elton had, in Percy Street, off Tottenham Court Road. It was also quite weird, because Ralph had kept his elderly man-servant, who would greet you formally while pushing aside the piece of three-ply that covered the entrance. Inside there were always mattresses on the floor, but, even in utter exhaustion, your sleep could be interrupted, as Ralph was mad about exotic pets, and had recently acquired a peccary, a strange South American pig, which crept out of the airing cupboard and snuffled at you in the most unexpected places.

My most frightening moment was when Chick Fowle and I spent the night on the top of the tower of the University building at Bloomsbury, then the highest building in the West End. As this area had been copping it pretty regularly, we hoped to get some spectacular stuff. To our disappointment, the raids that night were down in the City, and we were just packing up in disgust when there was a bloody great explosion in Tottenham Court Road, about 300 yards away. A land-mine, which came down by parachute, and therefore made no noise, had landed where Lyons Corner House used to be. After the bang, there was a second of silence, and then the crash of thousands of panes of glass, which because of the vacuum created always fell outwards. We were still pretty shaken when we suddenly heard 'whish-whish-whish!' It could only be another parachute! We flung ourselves down, but knew we'd had it. There was no condensed video flash of your past life, just the thought 'Fuck it, what bad luck'. Then, about four hundred pigeons, which had flown up from their roosting place in the British Museum just below where we were, landed all around us! We lay there for a long time, surrounded by agitated pigeons, before we had the strength to get up.

There was a typical blitz pay-off to that episode. Ralph Elton had been waiting for me at his flat, and when the bang came, decided to go out and look for me. He soon found a body without a face that he was sure was me, so 'Poor old Watty had bought it, let's drink to him', and he made his way to the Player's Club, in Albemarle Street, our other home from home where, during the war, Peter Ustinov, James Robertson Justice, Bernard Miles, and many others started their theatrical careers. Needing a drink badly, I also made my way there, and found everyone toasting my premature departure, and no doubt saying much nicer things about me than they ever said when I was alive. At least, I got a lot of free drinks.

By the end of five days and nights we had a mass of material, but this time it had been carefully shot to a shape. Each unit had been given its specific job, one covering people queueing for the buses and the shelters in ever darkening light, another ruined churches and historic buildings, another people in the shelters, anti-aircraft guns, and night blitz scenes. We also had units go out in the dawn to where the blitz had been worst, to cover the people struggling over the rubble to go to work, the rescues and the clearing up, and the improvised transport arrangements. I got a shot—which I admit I staged, but it often happened—of an immaculate civil servant, dressed like Anthony Eden, cadging a lift off a rag-and-bone man's cart. The civil servant was Julian Spiro's brother, Henry, a brilliant young man who was already a big-shot in Whitehall. He refused to accept his exemption from call-up, joined the Navy, and was drowned the first time he went to sea.

McAllister had been editing night and day while we were shooting, and had got a rough cut out, of reasonable shape, so I rushed off to the Ministry to see about a commentator. As the film was for America, I was sent to the American division and they suggested Mary Welsh, who later married Hemingway. They significantly said 'We know she's pro-British', confirming my suspicions about many of the American correspondents. I hate women commentators, and was sure our film would be ruined, so I begged Sidney Bernstein to suggest someone else. He said 'There's a big ex-pug staying at the Savoy, the *Collier's* man, who might be able to help you.' So off to the Savoy I go, and contact Quentin Reynolds, who was to be the first star created by documentary. He was an enormous, easy-going, rather drunken character, and a good journalist. He was eager to help, so we showed him the cutting-copy, gave him my treatment, and started him writing. It was a great advantage to us that he had never done any commentary writing before, as he wasn't possessive about his stuff, writing reams and letting us cut it and reject it as we wanted. However, he steadfastly refused to come out of the underground restaurant at the Savoy during the night, so I became, for the first time, a sudden *habitué* of that flash joint.

We took Quentin down to Denham to record the commentary. He had never even broadcast on radio, so we stood him in front of the mike and told him to have a go. The first words were 'I am speaking from London'. Quent bellowed them out like a barker in a fair-ground! I said 'That's great, Quent, great, but just take it down a bit, will you?' He did it again, and still sounded like a master of ceremonies at a banquet, so we gave him a drink, and got into a huddle in the sound booth. 'What in Christ's name are we going to do with this bloody awful bellowing bull?' Then Ken Cameron, the sound-man, had the flash of intuition that was to make Quentin Reynolds famous. He said 'Look, he's a big bugger with an enormous belly. Let's sit him down in an armchair, stick the microphone nearly down his throat, and let him whisper.' We did this, and rumbling out of that belly came the famous deep Quentin growl, that was destined to be listened to throughout the Allied world.

We were getting near our dateline, so we fixed a showing of the rough-cut film in London in two days' time. McAllister was so meticulous, insisting on making each word drop exact on the right visual shot, even the right half of the shot that we left Denham Studios with no time to spare and ran straight into a bad blitz. Arriving late, we found a few junior Ministry men nervously waiting in the private theatre of Humphries Laboratories obviously wanting to get back to their shelter as soon as possible. We put the film on double-headed, that is, the sound and the picture were on separate reels, and started off. It broke twice! This meant long delays, while the editor resynchronized it and rethreaded it onto the projectors. Our windy superiors were by now extremely agitated and when the film finally finished, scuttled out with hardly a word. Next day, our grapevine told us that the showing was being talked of in the coffee break at the film division, as 'last night's disaster'. By now we didn't give a damn, we could smell we had a good 'un, so pressed on with the final stages and arrived with an excellent married print for the Press Show. Quentin Reynolds had given us the title, *London Can Take It*. A lot of journalists turned up, including Arthur Christiansen, the editor of the *Daily Express*, and, at that time, Fleet Street's top man. After we'd run the film, he said emphatically 'That's the best war picture up to now' so we got marvellous notices. In no time the Ministry was going round saying 'Have you seen our new film?'

Christiansen invited Quent and me to lunch, and I asked if McAllister could come along. I had four day's growth of beard, and I don't think Mac had had any sleep for a week. When we got to Simpsons, Mac was delighted to see lobster soup on the menu, which he had read about but never tasted. It took a little time to come and the wait was too much for him. Just as the soup was served, poor old Mac crashed off his chair in a dead faint of pure exhaustion.

Quent was packed off to the States in a bomber with the film under his arm. Only Quent's name appeared on the titles, with no British credits at all, so all America imagined that this was an unbiased personal report made by one of their own people, a belief that Quent did not battle to belie. He toured America lecturing with the film at 750 dollars a time —a bit galling when the top whack at the Crown was ten quid a week—until Warner Brothers booked *London Can Take It* for nationwide release in their cinemas.

Quent returned, an international figure, and amused us by growling *sotto voce* all the time. What made us hoot with laughter was a poster for his lectures which he naïvely showed us. It depicted Quent gazing defiantly at the skies in a British tin-hat, and warding off, with his strong right arm, a five-hundred-pound bomb! It must have been a lot tougher in the Savoy Grill than we thought.

We laughed at Quent but he did a fine job of publicity for Britain when we needed it most. Goebbels had said that 'cinema was Germany's fourth offensive arm', and had used it brilliantly to frighten neutrals and convey an atmosphere of invincibility. Apart from Ed Murrow, Quent was the first outsider to speak up and say we would not be beaten. After he did his famous 'Mr Schickelgruber' broadcasts over here, he became a folk-hero, and walking down the street with him was like strolling with Cassius Clay today. He loved it, of course, and gave me a typically impractically-big, leather-covered flask, that held a quart, over which he had embossed: 'To Harry Watt, who made a ham out of me'. He was always a ham, all we did was make him a whispering one.

There was no let-up, of course, after our hectic fortnight. Suddenly there was an insatiable demand for films, instructional, educational, and straight propaganda. The commercial cinema had decided they must contribute, and weighed in with two outstanding stinkers. The first, *The Lion has Wings*, was made by Korda, and had no less than three directors, Michael Powell, Brian Desmond Hurst, and Adrian Brunel. A jumbled nothing, I can only remember they put Ralph Richardson in white overalls, so you knew he was the star. Vincent Sheean, the eminent American reporter, wrote from Germany that the Germans had got hold of a copy, and were running it in Berlin—as a comedy! The other was *Ships with Wings*, made at Ealing, and allegedly about the Fleet Air Arm, which so incensed Henry Spiro, soon to be killed in the Navy, that he sent a carefully worded telegram to the producer of the film, threatening to arrest him, and signed it The-Commander-in-Chief. There was only one good film made around that time, *49th Parallel*, but Eric Portman made such a powerful impression in the part of a German submarine commander on the run across Canada, that, to many, the film was better propaganda for the enemy than ourselves. An unsavoury episode was connected with this for Elizabeth Bergner, a German refugee and then a big star, refused to return from Canada after having been taken there for the exteriors of this film and all her scenes had to be reshot with Glynis Johns, costing, of course, a fortune, which the Ministry of Information paid for. Originally, on the outbreak of hostilities, the Ministry had closed the cinemas, but soon reopened them, realizing the necessity of relaxation and escape from the boredom of war. Our film-making industry having more or less collapsed, with call-ups, requisitions of studios, and general uncertainty, the Ministry encouraged and financed certain features, considered to be of national or artistic worth. They kept a reasonably tight control over the commercial film-makers throughout the war, with all productions having to be approved by them, and all film stock being rationed, both for features and newsreels.

I was involved in an episode around this time which showed how far apart commercial film-makers and documentary still were. A young feature film director, David MacDonald, suddenly blew in and asked if he could make a film with us. He had rocketed in reputation with two big successes, starring Alistair Sim, called *This Man is News* and *This Man in Paris*. As he was obviously sincere, and had chucked his job to come to us, Cavalcanti gave him a film we were working on about an episode off the Norfolk coast, where a lone German plane had brutally machine-gunned a lightship, presumably just for kicks. Lightships, like lighthouses, ambulances and so on, were supposed to be internationally sacrosanct. As the script was pretty well finished, Cav told Dave to go up to the lightship depot, and cast the film from the survivors and their mates. He was shocked, as he had presumed he could use actors. It was gently pointed out to him that we could not afford actors, and the budget was mentioned, which was about what he had earned in a month. He then said he knew every small-part character man in the business and could find, around Charing Cross Road, a bunch of chaps who would cost peanuts and act like Spencer Tracy. Cavalcanti let him have his way. So after kitting his gang out at Berman's the costumiers, Dave set off for the east coast. About a week later, a worried Cavalcanti asked me, although I had nothing to do with the film, to have a look at the rushes. Dave's doughties were quite ghastly. To start with, they were dressed up. A fisherman's cap or jersey has got to be worn for about ten years before it looks right. Then they couldn't row properly —they were supposed to be escaping in their small boat— and went in and out of it like a bunch of arthritics. Finally, their faces were worn with drink and late nights, not with the sea and the wind. They were soft, that was what was mainly the matter with them, they were soft.

Cav and I just looked at each other, shook our heads, and he took the first train east and fired the lot. I must say Dave took it well, recast with the real people and battled through the film, which came out well under the title *Men of the Lightships*. He then went off to join the Army Film Unit, of which he became head, and a colonel.

There had been suggestions, from time to time, that we should be mobilized, and put in uniform, as we were working more and more with the Services. We resisted this partly because there was basically no rank in our communally run unit—although there was excellent discipline on the job—partly because we were such a scruffy mob we would have been sure to clash with the spit and polishers, but also—and much more importantly—we knew that as soon as some of us became officers we could no longer make our type of films. As civilians, we could talk on equal terms with all ranks, from the Top Brass to the lowest 'erk', and get our dialogue and scripts from these conversations. It would have been the old class thing again, which we had spent ten years trying to cut through. Sweet old Cav rather fancied himself as a 'Col-on-el' for a while, but we pulled his leg so much that he soon forgot about it.

I made a routine picture on training the auxiliary police, called *Law and Order*, in which there was one good joke, and then the Ministry insisted that Quentin Reynolds and I make a successor to *London Can Take It*. Neither of us wanted to do it, as we knew how difficult it is to follow a big success. However, as they said what was needed was something to make the American public uncomfortable while they celebrated Christmas, we decided, very much tongue in cheek, to make a weepy. Our private motto was 'Not a dry seat in the house'. We called it *Christmas Under Fire*, and the first shuddering line was 'The Christmas trees will have to be very small this year, to fit into the air raid shelters'. It may have disturbed the gorging Yanks, but no more than it did us when we ran it. The Ministry was delighted and apparently it was very successful.

*   *   *   *   *

It was shortly after this that I had my best idea of the war. I went to the Ministry and asked why couldn't we make a hitting back film, instead of these interminable 'taking it' efforts. We were already starting to bomb Germany, so there was the obvious subject. The Ministry agreed wholeheartedly, so off I went to see the Air Force Public Relations Officer, a Wing-Commander Williams, one of my most unfavourite characters. His usual ploy was to say 'OK, old boy, come down around twelve, will you?', and then immediately suggest a recess to the nearest pub, where the conference continued, over double gins, until three o'clock. I hated drinking in the middle of the day, and it took three weeks of sore heads and frustration, before I got anything moving at all. Then Williams produced, from the bowels of the Air Ministry, where presumably he had been ciphering or decoding, a Pilot Officer Derek Twist, who had been something in the film business, to act as my conducting officer. Being a dirty civilian, I could not be trusted to introduce myself to aerodromes by myself. (In fact, this move did Derek Twist, a charming chap, a power of good, because he escaped permanently from his bunker and became head of the Air Force Film Unit.)

I was taken to the supposedly very secret headquarters of Bomber Command, which, to my utter astonishment, I found to be a few miles from where my wife and son were evacuated. It was extremely difficult not to mention at home that I had passed that way the day before, but at least I knew why our windows and doors kept getting blown in.

I decided to make the film at Mildenhall Aerodrome, near Newmarket, where 149 Squadron was stationed, because the CO and the Group Commander were eager and interested. Then began the long journalist-cum-detective work necessary to get a really authentic script. I read over two thousand pilots' raid reports. Ninety-odd per cent of them just said 'Took off, bombed target, little—or lot of—flak', and left it at that, but a few, with perhaps, literary aspirations, gave descriptions of exciting or memorable moments, and these I tucked away to use later. I hung around the aerodrome for a month, trying to be as inconspicuous as possible, but talking to everyone. It developed into gin with the officers, beer with the sergeants, and mammoth mugs of tea with the maintenance crews in the dispersal huts. I attended every briefing, and sat behind Wing-Commander Powell, the CO, when he was giving his last whoop talks to 'sprog' crews, that is, new-comers straight from training, going off on their first bombing raid. I can see them now, those eager fresh-faced kids, from all over the Commonwealth, fidgeting and grinning nervously as they listened to the banal words of encouragement. I can see them because I followed the CO into the operations room and waited and waited, and prayed for their return. Almost inevitably, it was the beginners who copped it. Gradually the entries on the blackboard were filled up as the squadron straggled home, until there would be one blank space left as dawn began to rise. And it wasn't the blank space you saw, but those young, so terribly young, faces, lovely faces, that you knew were lying somewhere burnt and smashed.

Having finished my script, and had it passed as technically correct—very important when working with the Services—I set about casting. I had of necessity to use all the senior officers as they came, but I needed the crew of one bomber, to follow throughout the picture. The story was, again, utterly straightforward, just the choice of a new small target, the selection of a squadron to bomb it, and the adventures of one bomber, 'F for Freddie', during the raid.

I picked, as the captain of the bomber, and the key figure in the film, Squadron Leader Freddie Pickard, who happened to be the brother-in-law of Sir Cedric Hardwicke, but who had never acted. He was a large blond, easy-going individual, older than the others at twenty-four, and, as a flyer, as mad as a hatter. His favourite trick was to make the film crew throw themselves flat in the dust as he buzzed us with the Tiger Moth he scooted around in. He was actually in charge of a Czech Squadron on a nearby satellite aerodrome, and had endeared himself to them forever by a typical gesture on the night of their first operational mission. Lord Haw-Haw had announced on the radio that any Poles or Czechs captured from aeroplanes flying over Germany would immediately be shot. When Pick, who was leading the raid, came down to supper, it was suddenly spotted that he had 'Czechoslovakia' flashes sewn on his uniform.

Pick, 'Speedy' Powell the CO, and most of the crew of 'F for Freddie' were killed before the war was out.

I sent for my faithful little unit, Jonah Jones and Julian Spiro, and we started shooting the many essential atmosphere and cut-in shots around the aerodrome before starting the story proper. It had become very hot, so after about ten hours on the boiling tarmac, we used to head for the officers' mess for a couple of beers. I suddenly got a message to report to Wing-Commander Williams at Air Ministry by ten next morning. I had the usual hellish wartime train journey into an air raid, wondering all the time if the film had been cancelled. When I got to the Air Ministry, Williams started 'Something very serious has been reported to me, which could well jeopardize the whole project.' I racked my brains. Security? Jokes about the big shots? But it sounded bloody serious. Williams went on 'It has been reported to me that you and your unit consistently enter the officers' mess at Mildenhall in open-necked shirts, without even a tie.' As God is my witness he said that, in the middle of the war! It was a good thing he went on, before I could let fly with what was on the tip of my tongue. 'If this sort of behaviour continues, we'll have to consider whether you are the right sort of people to make the film.' I took it, because I wanted to make the picture, but that wasn't all I was to have to take from the bastard.

We decided to shoot all the interiors in a studio, but most of them were too ambitious for our little Blackheath Hall, so we did them at Elstree or Denham. As this was very expensive for us, we had to schedule carefully for maximum speed. I had, of course, brought my air-crew to London and they were working out marvellously. Apart from Pick, I had a Scotsman, an Australian, a Canadian, and two other Englishmen, one of whom, incidentally, had been a footman at 10 Downing Street, and had that address still on his driving licence, which, he claimed, helped enormously when he had trouble with the police.

Came the day when we were all set up to start, in one of Elstree's smallest stages, on the changing-room scenes, where the crews get into their flying gear before being taken by lorry to their respective aircraft. Wing-Commander Williams was to provide thirty more personnel to be a milling background to the foreground dialogue of our crew. By nine o'clock we had rehearsed the dialogue and lit the set, but no extras had appeared. I got on the telephone to Williams, and he had forgotten all about it! 'Very sorry, but frightfully busy, old boy'—I waited for him to say 'There's a war on, you know,' but luckily he didn't—'I'll get on to Three Group and they'll let us have some chaps in a couple of days'. A couple of days, at two hundred quid a day—not on your Nellie! I smashed the phone down and ran to find Julian Spiro. Within half an hour he had hired a bus, and set off for nearby Uxbridge, a big RAF recruiting depot. He stood in the main street, accosting wandering airmen like a tout for a Mystery Tour, and offered them five bob and a free lunch to appear in a film. Uxbridge High Street has few attractions to hold anyone even in peacetime, so Julian was soon back with a full load of bewildered AC2's. Luckily, we had plenty of flying kit, so they were soon pulling on wool-lined boots and shapeless padded suits, and no doubt dreaming of the time when they would be doing it in earnest. Strangely enough, the scenes came out full of atmosphere, and as realistic as any in the film.

Then we came to our big scene. It was on a full stage at Denham and was, I think, the biggest set ever built by documentary. It was a replica of the operations room at Bomber Command, much enlarged, and with double the number of bomber squadrons mentioned around the walls than in fact Britain possessed. By enormous persuasion, including showing the material already photographed, we had persuaded the Commander-in-Chief, Sir Richard Pierce, DSO, AFC, to appear in person. He had finally agreed to give us one hour exactly, while, presumably, the air war stopped.

The big day came. I was in my suit, we had scouts out along the approach road with signal flags to warn us of the approaching cavalcade, everything had been prepared, the set was pre-lit. The C-in-C brought with him so much brass it looked like the signing of a Peace Treaty. Army liaison officers, Naval liaison officers, and the lowest form of air officer was a Commodore. Naturally, Williams was there, saluting and bobbing and bottom-kissing.

We led the great man onto the set, which he duly praised, and I explained that he had to sit at his desk, look at the aerial photos and intelligence reports which we had already described in the film, and, swinging round on his chair, say to his second in command 'Yes, I agree these are interesting. Put a squadron on to bomb it tonight.' (We were then to follow what those few casual words meant to six ordinary Air Force bods.)

Owing to the time limit, we decided to shoot right away. The old boy did it perfectly, but as he swung round in his chair, there came from it a tooth-edging screech, the kind one sometimes hears from the axle of a mule cart in the remoter parts of Italy. The propmen were in like a shot 'Don't worry, guv, sort it aht in a minute, guv, drop of oil, that's all it needs, guv', and proceeded to squirt oil in all directions. The C-in-C did his stuff again, and the squeak was worse! Two hours later we got the shot, and it was three hours before we got his nibs away. He had become so film struck that it didn't seem to matter, so I presume the Germans slept in their beds that night.

We had now only the main sequence to shoot, the interior of the actual aircraft, and I had asked my dear friend, Wing-Commander Williams, to supply me with the fuselage of a crashed Wellington bomber. Pranged aircraft were one of the more common phenomena of south-east England at that time, and dotted the landscape like molehills. Any one of us could have told him where half a dozen Wellingtons lay. But it had to go through 'the proper channels', so we kicked our heels for three weeks. The boys had a great time in London—we were strictly instructed not to pay them extra, but they naturally needed pocket money—yet even they were getting bored when a spanking new Wellington fuselage drew into Denham on a low-loader. I had specifically asked for a really clapped-out job, so that we could tear it to pieces, but this was ours to do what we liked with, so we proceeded to cut it up and get our cameras and lights inside. We had been filming happily for about a week, when an RAF chap, who had wandered onto the set, drew me aside and said 'That black box, just back of the pilot's seat, do you know what it is?' I replied 'Haven't the faintest—can't understand half of those knobs and things.' He then looked around in the conventional mysterious manner and said 'If I were you, I'd have it unscrewed right away and put in the safe'. It turned out to be one of Britain's newest secret weapons, an anti-radar device, with a self-destructive charge included. Williams had excelled himself but I don't imagine anyone carried the can.

We had an excellent musical score written by Leighton Lucas, who was in the RAF. McAllister did his usual superb job of cutting and we informed the Ministry that the film was finished. It is interesting, in retrospect, that we had no belief we had 'a good 'un' in *Target for Tonight*—we nearly called it F for Freddie—as we had had for *London Can Take It*. There had been so many delays and frustrations, and we had been so close for so long to the desperate reality of the bombing campaign, that it appeared to us just an ordinary account of a minor operation.

The Ministry informed us that there would be a Press Show on such and such a day at 12.30 pm in the Cambridge Theatre. What they did not know, being completely unskilled in such things, was that on that same day, at 10.30 am, an important American company was showing one of their features—with free drinks afterwards! Drinks—particularly free ones—were hard to come by in those days, so when 12.30 came, I sat there in the large empty theatre, with my little unit, a couple of Ministry chaps, and an elderly usherette. I rushed down to the foyer and looked anxiously up the road. Not a newspaperman in sight. By twenty-to-one about four critics, rather flushed, strolled in, looked at their watches, and said 'OK, Harry, let's see your picture' (it was kind of them not to say 'little picture'). I stalled desperately, but when another two appeared and complained, I started the showing. While the film was running, the rest of the newspaper crowd drifted in, including my friend and mentor, Arthur Christiansen, of the *Express*. When the lights went up, although it was now about one-thirty, Chris said in a loud voice 'That looks like a damn good picture to me, I'd like to see the beginning. Will you run it again, Harry?' In Fleet Street, Chris was a law unto himself. I was off to the projection box like a rocket, and nobody left the theatre. I believe *Target for Tonight* is the only film ever to be run twice at a Press Show.

It is difficult for me to tell the staggering impact *Target for Tonight* had. To start with, there is the obvious danger of sounding as though one is just blowing one's own trumpet. But I can say that, while the film was honest and well made, it was no cinematic revolution, but an understated and unemotional account of an average air raid. To give the real reason for its success one must realize the emotions of the people of this country at the moment it came out. All propaganda had been geared to encourage us to bear up, to stay cheerful and optimistic under bombs, mines, torpedoes, rationing and cold, while a constant stream of success stories came from the other side. There was no sign of cracking, but I believe, away back in many people's minds, there had arisen the doubt that we could ever win, although I am sure we would have fought to the end. Then came this film, actually showing how we were taking the war into the heart of the enemy, and doing it in a very British, casual, brave way. It was a glimmer of hope, and the public rose to it. It was the luck of the moment at which it appeared that brought about its stupendous success. I have always said I had more luck than talent.

Statistics are boring, but *Target for Tonight* ran at three large West End cinemas simultaneously, while its story was being serialized in the *Daily Express*, billed as 'The Greatest Story of the War'. Charles Oakley, in his authoritative book on the history of British cinema, *Where We Came In*, says: 'In the course of a few months the film was shown in over 12,000 theatres in the United States, Canada and South America, and was seen by 50 million people.' This does not, I imagine, include the blanket exhibition it received in Britain, where the phrase *Target for Tonight* became a national catchword. A comedian had only to look at a pretty chorus-girl and say 'Target for Tonight' to get a howl of laughter and a round of applause. The nadir of the exploitation of the title came when an insecticide manufacturer showed a picture of an enormous bed-bug, and printed 'Target for Tonight' beneath it.

The film was distributed commercially by the Ministry, but at a cheap rate, say twenty per cent of the take, instead of the more usual forty to fifty per cent. As my physical costs were only around £6,000, it must have made as big a profit as any famous feature film. Strangely enough, I have never been able to find out anything about the money side of *Target*. This, I imagine, is because, while the Ministry distributed the film, the receipts went direct to the Treasury. Although I believe it was dubbed in America, where they still found English accents incomprehensible, and this, no doubt, cost a bit, the return from all those cinemas must have been pretty colossal. Incidentally, it also won a wartime Oscar in America, which I never even saw, and Aimee Semple MacPherson, the famous evangelist in Hollywood, ran it during one of her meetings, and then preached on the theme 'Jesus is our Target for Tonight'.

The pay-off for me—if it can be called that, for it was a disaster—came with a phone call before *Target* had hit the cinemas. Would I go to Claridges Hotel and look up Mr Merian C. Cooper? I had never been in Claridges, he was obviously an American, so at least there would be plenty of booze, and off I trotted. I was shown up to this enormous suite, in which there was an old boy in red braces, with a five-gallon hat lying on the couch. He went into the patter about liking my pictures, and then said he represented Walter Wanger, the Hollywood producer, who was going to make a film about the Eagle Squadron, and would I direct it? I had better explain that the Eagle Squadron was the one in Fighter Command manned exclusively by young American flyers, who had made their way over by various and sometimes devious means and volunteered to fight. I happened to know most of them well, as RAF pay being what it was, it could hardly keep Yanks in fags, so they had had a standing invitation from the war correspondents at the Savoy to eat and drink there whenever they were on leave.

I explained to Cooper that I was mobilized into Government service, but he just waved a hand casually and said he'd already fixed all that. I was flattered and tempted, because I liked the boys immensely, and here was an unusual way to make a film about fighters, which I had often wanted to do. So I said if it really was OK by the Ministry, I'd have a go. Cooper then gave me an enormous Scotch, and asked me did I want to talk money then, or let my agent handle it? Luckily I had not yet drunk the Scotch, so mumbled quickly that my agent would get in touch with him. I, of course, had never had an agent in my life, but I remembered I used to write to Robert Flaherty care of one, so I shot downstairs to a telephone and told this agent that some Yank called Cooper wanted me to make a picture, and to get me a good deal. As the most I'd ever earned had been thirty quid a week for a short time on *Jamaica Inn*, and as I was accustomed and reconciled to my ten quid Crown salary, what he got me knocked me sideways. A hundred a week, plus free living at the Savoy!

Cooper went back, and I started shooting atmosphere stuff down at the Eagle Squadron base in Essex. The boys welcomed me, as we were pals, and I could lash out with the expenses, but, although they were a wild bunch, they were highly professional and disciplined on the job, extremely proud of being in the RAF and as zealous of its tradition and reputation as any regular. (Indeed, when the few survivors were finally transferred to the American Air Force, they refused to wear their RAF medal ribbons behind their American ones, as they were supposed to do, British medals being rated as foreign decorations. They knew they had gained their 'gongs' the hard way, and, as one succinctly remarked to me later on, they felt that 'the Americans give you some sort of medal if you get a dose of clap'.)

The aerial tactics of that moment were low-level bomb attacks on French communications, with fighter cover, of which the Eagle Squadron was part. It was chancy work, because the Germans had still a lot of fighters in the Low Countries, and were always liable to jump you out of the sun. The Americans, and there were only twenty-four of them, were already beginning to have casualties, so I could not concentrate on any particular individuals.

Then the associate producer, or so he called himself, turned up. He was the all-time creep. This is almost unbelievable, but this young greaseball had ingratiated himself in some way to Walter Wanger, and had never been in the film business! His first job was to take a big suite, have it furnished with a double-sized double-bed—no kidding—acquire a flossy chick, and tell me to get on with it! He obviously had plenty of gall, because when I explained about the casualties in the Eagle Squadron, he went off to the Air Ministry and requested that the squadron should be withdrawn from the front line while we make the film! (This is true, but there was a possibly apocryphal story that another American producer offered the British Government a million dollars for exclusive rights on the invasion.) The Air Ministry politely told him where he could go, so he came back to me and said we'd just have to make the film with the squadron where it was. I asked. 'What about the script?' He then told me to just shoot it like *Target*, which they obviously imagined had somehow been shot off the cuff! I refused to shoot without a script, so he told me to write one.

Then followed four weeks of the most utter chaos I have ever been involved in. Apart from trying to write the script, and shoot scrambles, take-offs and landings, etc, down in Essex, I was suddenly engulfed in the notoriety of the success of *Target*. It was all too much for me and for the first and only time in my life I went on the town, which, from hazy memory, seemed to be just going from one seedy night-club to another. Such was the impact of *Target*, that, when one of my party whispered to the MC who I was, the spotlight would swing onto me, and the MC announce 'Tonight, ladies and gentlemen, we have with us the man who made *Target for Tonight!*', and a free bottle of champagne would arrive. Heady stuff for a youngster with no particularly strong moral fibre, and it nearly finished me.

Luckily, I was still a dedicated film-maker, and could see disaster looming for the Eagle Squadron production, so I went off to see George Archibald, now Lord Archibald, the then head of United Artists, who were handling the cash. I told him I wanted to chuck my hand in right away, and, to my considerable astonishment, he begged me to stay, saying 'I think you're the sanest of the whole bunch.' To me, who was generally looked on as one of the craziest in a crazy business, this was a most unexpected compliment, but it showed what he thought of the whole project.

I returned to the dreariness of success and heaven knows what would have happened, if it all had not been tragically resolved one Black Sunday. I had gone down to the Eagle Squadron's base, just for a chat and a drink, but soon twelve planes were called away to act as top cover to a raid. It soon became obvious that something ominous was happening over France. The boys had been jumped, and, of the twelve, three battered planes staggered home. Most of the rest were dead, including my closest friend. He was the last of a trio of gay, careless adventurers whom I had become very attached to, in the casual ephemeral way these things happen in wartime. After a good deal of hesitation, I wrote the following epitaph to them.

I Had Three Friends

I had three friends: Andy, Shorty and Red. Three young Americans of the type you see in those films of college life and wonder if they really exist. Handsome young animals with curly hair and magnificent teeth. Who talk a lot in a vivid cynical vernacular that belies the sentimentality beneath.

Andy was massive and broad. A Russian type with pale blue eyes in a puckish Mongol face. Shorty was a tiny dynamo, with a shock of fair hair and an Irish temperament.

Red was perhaps the most typical young American of the three. Tall and lanky, he had a grin that split his face in two and a devastating vocabulary of wisecracks that was the delight of his friends, and the despair of his seniors.

Way back in 1940, when America was hardly conscious that World War II had begun, these three sneaked across the Canadian border to fly for democracy.

They loved telling how they fooled the G-men who at that time were trying to stop them, by saying they were going to visit a cousin who kept a trout hatchery. None of them could ever explain why a 'trout hatchery'.

And while France was beginning to fall, the three were fighting the smells in a mule boat crossing the Atlantic. They landed at Cherbourg to join the Escadrille Lafayette, just as the might of Germany began to sweep across France. And for a month their lives were a series of crazy adventures.

They went from airfield to airfield only to see the aircraft they were to fly 'tomorrow' bombed out of existence. They saw the Stukas come over in hordes, while the French fighter pilots shrugged their shoulders and left their aircraft to their fate.

With some Czechs they tried to steal an airplane and

had to run for their lives with machine-gun bullets zipping through the trees behind them. And all the time they kept their incredible American enjoyment of life. When you used to ask them of their time in France their usual reply was simply 'Aw, hell, we had a million laughs.'

Shorty thought it was undignified to fight a war without uniform and used to march up to every senior French Officer he saw and, in the most incredible French, demand one. Although it was patiently explained that no-one was bothering to hand out uniforms any more, and anyway there wasn't one small enough to fit him, he persisted. He never even got a pair of flying boots.

In every town they went to Andy found a French girl he wanted to marry. And although he never could describe them very well, as he'd always met them in the black-out, his heart-throbs caused quite a bit of trouble to the other two.

And all the time Red the imperturbable would act as general provider. What he couldn't scrounge, he'd wheedle, using a weird combination of signs, grins and bad French, even once throwing in a song-and-dance routine as good measure. He always got what he wanted.

They soon realized the game was up in France, so they hopped a train to the south. It was a freight train, and the wagons were full of bags of a yellowish dust that got on their clothes and clogged their eyes and hair.

But they stubbed their cigarettes on the sacks and thought no more about it. It wasn't until the morning that a Frenchman explained that the yellow powder was high explosive! He demonstrated with a handful on the side of the line. It blew Andy's hat off. So after that they walked.

The three musketeers came to England in the last ship out of St Jean de Luz, and went straight to the American Embassy in London. They had vague ideas that they might be treated as heroes.

Instead they were treated as civil servants treat adventurers the world over. They were classified. They were classified as 'distressed American nationals' and ordered home. When they talked about fighting they were blasted by phrases like 'jeopardizing neutrality'. They came out into the street feeling pretty sick.

157

But they'd heard about this country. They'd heard about a place called the House of Parliament. And one even had an introduction to a member of that House.

So the three American kids, who only wanted to fight and fly against the Germans, and who had found it the most difficult job of their lives, went up to a London bobby and asked him if he knew a place called the House of Parliament.

And the bobby in his tin hat and gas mask looked at their tattered and dirty store clothes and no doubt thought it was a funny time and way to sight-see. But he directed them.

Off the three went, and it is to the eternal credit of the unknown MP that within a day they were in the RAF.

It was at the time when every flier was needed. With only the shortest of training the three Americans were posted to the famous 609 Squadron, and they flew with them throughout the whole of that fateful autumn, the only Americans to fight in the Battle of Britain.

They were the new boys of the squadron and as such became the 'tail-end Charlies'. Day after day, while the Germans were throwing their whole aerial might against us, Andy, Shorty and Red weaved and wisecracked at the tail of their squadron, protecting their British comrades from surprise attack.

They had all the fighting they wanted. And they acquitted themselves well. Red shot down a Dornier and a Messerschmitt. Andy got a couple of Heinkels. Shorty got in among a bunch of the enemy and shot up three before being shot down himself. He landed, full of holes, in a field and cursed for ten minutes.

Red, who never missed a chance to take a crack at Shorty's size, asked him if he had the wind up. Shorty looked for a chair to stand on to hit Red on the nose. The three were inseparable.

The Battle of Britain was won. And the three Americans of 609 Squadron, who had done nothing spectacular, nothing sensational, except take their honourable place beside the boys of the Empire and the homeland who saved the nation, were sent to form the nucleus of the first all-American squadron to fight with us—the Eagle Squadron.

Now the Eagle Squadron is in our front line. It flies over occupied France every day in the Battle of Germany. It is building up a fine record. Two of its members have received the DFC.

But my three friends are not with it any more. Shorty got into a spin while chasing a hit-and-run Heinkel, and failed to pull out. Red went in behind Boulogne while fighting off half a dozen Messerschmitts. Andy hit a hill while making a reconnaissance flight in bad weather.

My three friends died as they expected to die, flying for Britain. As Red used to say with a grin, as he pointed to the wings on his chest, 'This is a one-way ticket, pal.' Andy, Shorty and Red were the pioneers. There are now three American squadrons flying with our Fighter Command and more to come.

I am proud to have had those three friends.

There was a rather macabre sequel to the publishing of that article by the *Daily Express* in November 1941. I was suddenly rung up by an excited Cockney voice who, after introducing himself—which I didn't catch—went on something like this: 'It's great, absolutely great, be a world-wide hit, I've got the boys working on the music now, what a title eh? "I Had Three Friends", biggest thing since "Wing and a Prayer", fifty-fifty eh?' I then grasped that this was a Charing Cross Road music publisher, who wanted to turn my story into a sob ballad. I was revolted. I had only written the article after asking the boys of the Eagle Squadron if they minded. But I definitely did not want it drooled around the world by a ghoul behind a microphone. I said no at once. The little man was shocked. He started quoting figures at me, which, if true, were pretty impressive. I shut him up by saying I did not own the copyright, phoned up Christiansen, who agreed at once not to release it under any circumstances, and that was that. I wonder if the parents of my three pals, who were simple American folk, might not have enjoyed their boys' sacrifice being perpetuated in song, no matter how banal. But I know the boys would have hated it.

The Eagle Squadron film was finished in Hollywood with actors, but I never saw it.

I returned joyfully to Crown, and within a day, found myself and Chick Fowle humping camera gear up the face of a quarry. I suddenly stopped and panted 'Boy, this is the life—great, isn't it?' Chick, who like all the Unit had imagined my fling into the high-life must have been heaven, gave me a quizzical Cockney look, as though to say 'Phoney bastard', and merely asked me to hand him a magazine. But, for once, I was being completely genuine.

6

I found a lot happening back in the Unit. Jack Holmes, after making a first-class 'taking it' film, *Ordinary People*, which sadly suffered the fate of *Squadron 992*, was soon to be off making *Coastal Command*. Humphrey Jennings, the unrepentant intellectual, was really in his stride, and starting on a picture of the Fire Service. Pat Jackson was making *Ferry Pilot*, and Julian Spiro went to America to make *We Sail at Midnight*. But I was shattered and depressed by the loss of my sweet Cavalcanti, who had left to join Ealing Studios. I could understand why, of course, because his position as a foreigner had always been a bit invidious, his mother was now elderly, and he had hankered after some luxury before it was too late. I missed him tremendously, because I knew that I would never have achieved anything without his kindly, tortuous, but always practical advice. I would like to say that, while the idea and inspiration of the British documentary movement came from Grierson, its style and quality came from Cavalcanti.

Jack Holmes and I tried to cope with the administration and production work, but I, particularly, was utterly unsuited to a desk job, so we decided to call in, as producer, Ian Dalrymple, who had been a successful features film editor, and seemed sympathetic and practical. I was not to realize it at first, but his coming meant the end of the road for me in documentary.

I looked around for a new subject, and, unexpectedly, found it difficult. By this time, the Services had expanded their Film Units enormously, and were beginning to cover their own action stuff all over the world. However, a new élite force, the Commandos, was getting a lot of publicity, and I asked if I could make a film about them. The War Office agreeing, I went off to various training grounds in the west of Scotland. Although the training was fierce, and the men the pick of the Army, it was what one was already seeing in newsreels, and, no matter how much it could be jazzed up with explosions, machine-gun sounds and so on, it was basically phoney. So I said I couldn't write a script without seeing some real action, and when would that happen, please? I naturally got flat military stares in reply, but I suddenly received a phone call to report to Whitehall, where I was made a War Correspondent, and told to go to some obscure suburb to be kitted out. I hadn't worn uniform since my short-lived and somewhat unfortunate period in the Edinburgh University OTC, so was rather lost about what went where. I wasn't given time to experiment, as that night I left for Aberdeen, in a train apparently occupied solely by Army officers, who all seemed to be watching me with sardonic amusement. The climax came when I reported to a transit camp near Aberdeen. An enormous Scots sergeant gave me a magnificent salute with his 'Good evening, Captain Watt'. His expression of disgust when he realized he had given of his best to 'some bluidy reporter' was beautiful to behold.

I was soon shipped to Scapa Flow, in the Orkneys, and joined Number Three Commando on one of two converted cross-channel steamers. I was made very welcome and soon felt at home, as smartness and spit and polish did not rank high in Commando's priorities. The officers, apart from the CO, Colonel Durnford-Slater, were young, tremendously keen, but not conspicuously intelligent. The men were as tough a bunch as I had ever come across, many of whom had obviously found the discipline of conventional regiments too irksome to take. They were hard to control, but what soldiers they made.

I was joined by my cameraman, Harry Rignold, from the Army Film Unit. Harry had been with us at the GPO, but opted to go into the Army, and was, I think, their first official photographer. He was one of those unexpected heroic figures that Britain seems to throw up in wartime. Born 'in a theatrical basket', as the saying is, he toured the music-halls most of his youth with his parents' variety act. He was a tiny, dapper little man, who seemed to love uniforms, and, when on leave, always put on the works, gleaming like the juvenile lead in a wartime musical comedy. Yet he was one of the bravest

162

men I have ever known, standing up and calmly filming while everyone else was cowering in slit trenches. He was given the Military Cross in North Africa—a decoration only given for bravery under fire—and was killed at Anzio.

It was now late November and the weather was foul. It was obvious we were planning a raid on Norway, but no-one knew where and the constant speculation kept us alert. The Commandos went off in landing craft and rehearsed daily, while there were endless liaison meetings with the Air Force and the Navy. There had already been a small raid on the Lofoten Islands, but that had almost been a farce, and the total bag was about half a dozen frightened German meteorologists. This was obviously going to be a bigger affair, because there were more Commandos in the other ship, and a detachment of the Free Norwegian Forces. There also appeared on that ship a crew from the Army Film Unit, and a newsreel man, while we were joined by an agency reporter. He was to do the story for all the newspapers.

All the originals were getting pretty edgy—we were kept completely incommunicado for nearly two months, only being allowed to write those measly Services printed cards, where you scratch out the words that don't apply—when it was announced that we were going to attack Vaagso, a small town in northern Norway, on Christmas Day, a sweet little Commando idea to catch the German garrison bloated and asleep. Vaagso lay far up a long narrow fjord, and was reputed to be defended by about two hundred Germans, plus a battery of coastal guns on a small island just beyond the entrance to the harbour. It was a tough target.

Just before we were due to leave we were visited by Lord Louis Mountbatten, newly appointed Head of Combined Operations. He was perfect type-casting, with the classic profile, the lean figure, the medals, and enough gold braid to dazzle the eye. We were all assembled in the ship's saloon, where he gave us an excellent short whoop-talk. Colonel Durnford-Slater was just drawing breath to say 'Three cheers for Lord Louis Mountbatten' when one of the soldiers at the back shouted, with a lovely raucous Cockney voice, 'What abaht the bloody grub?' He didn't care about making a gesture for democracy, about showing our gallant allies that the lion had teeth, that we were beginning to force the Nazi heel from the neck of their victims, his only worry was his belly. I'm afraid I disgraced myself by laughing.

We left in convoy with three destroyers and a light cruiser, HMS *Kenya*, and ran into a gale. As we kept going at full speed, our vessel shipped so much water we had to put into somewhere in the Shetlands to pump out her forepeak. That day's delay may have cost us many lives. I used the time to shoot some preliminary stuff, with the help of a Commando officer with whom I had become very friendly, a young Australian called Bill Lloyd. He was extremely handsome, and, it gradually turned out, very rich. He was fascinated with the film business, and we had spent many hours speculating and planning what we could do together after the war.

The storm died suddenly and we set off, straight across for Norway, in almost a flat calm. It was still dark when a loom appeared on the horizon and the knowledge that this was enemy country gave one a flutter in the stomach. In the blink of dawn, we had approached close enough to see the high ominous cliffs guarding the frighteningly narrow fjord. A periscope—one of ours, thank God—suddenly surfaced ahead of us and led us in, like a friendly porpoise. The scheme was that the RAF was to put on a diversionary bombing raid, and that we would make our way up the fjord during this to a position about a mile from Vaagso, where everyone would leave the depot ships in landing craft. Half would make for the town itself, landing on a beach nearby, and the other half make for the fortified island with the big guns. If we got within striking distance of our objectives without detection, the Colonel was to fire ten red Verey lights, and the planes were to abandon their phoney raid, swoop down to us, and drop smoke canisters to cover our actual landing.

We crept onto our embarkation point and set off in the landing craft. Harry Rignold and I went towards the town, because that was our mob's objective. The other film people went to the island, on paper the tougher assignment, but, by the luck of the draw, we saw ninety per cent of the action.

As we set off in the barges we could see the German ack-ack, sited on the cliff tops, streaking up at the British planes, and realized how easy it would be for them to shoot us to pieces

164

if we were spotted. As always, some Scot had smuggled his pipes aboard, and the thin weird music, the music that has led men to war over so many centuries, encouraged us as we sat, huddled and cold, in the crowded craft. The piper was Major Jack Churchill, one of the most astounding characters to come out of the war. Although trained as a regular Army officer, he was perfect Commando material. He went into every battle with his pipes, and led his men with a claymore, the traditional Scottish broadsword. After Vaagso, he fought on various fronts until he landed up with the partisans in Yugoslavia, still complete with bagpipes.

As soon as we were well on our way, the cruiser moved into the centre of the fjord, and, after a sighting salvo of flares, poured broadside after broadside into the island. With this whistling over our heads, we were soon within about 500 yards of our objectives, and the first red Verey light went up. The shelling stopped, and we were suddenly very aware of the loud throb of our engines. As the Verey lights followed each other lazily into the sky, our six boats broke from the rest and headed hard for the land. Now we could hear the drone of our bombers high overhead change to a scream as they dived right at us, and roared in at almost sea-level, to drop their smoke canisters, great dustbins full of sulphur and potassium, on the beach-head.

The little beach we were rushing at disappeared in a cloud of thick choking white smoke, as the planes clawed back off the cliffs and started their second run. Then our first tragedy happened. Perhaps deceived by the smoke, or harassed by the intense ack-ack fire from the Germans, one of the planes dropped its canister straight into the landing craft next to ours. As it exploded, it showered its dreadful contents over everyone, a spluttering white-hot lava that ate through clothing like a cigarette through paper. Several soldiers and the naval engineer were killed and the rest leapt into the water. We, in our craft, knew little of all this, because by now we were in the smoke, firing was coming from the shore ahead where the first boats had landed, and all around were yells, screams, orders, gunfire, aeroplane noise and general pandemonium. And then we ran aground! The very young officer in charge dropped the landing platform that made up the bow of the barge, and roared 'All out, come on, all out'. The Commandos disappeared into the water and the smoke, now thicker than a London pea-souper, leaving me and Harry Rignold, who had the camera and tripod. I was draped all over with magazine boxes, and—quite illegally—a rifle. The snotty was getting hysterical, 'Come on, you two, for Christ's sake, jump.' Harry disappeared, but I hung back. One of the secrets that I am ashamed of is that I can't swim. With that and about fifty pounds of assorted ironmongery attached to my person, I was naturally reluctant. I said, rather coyly, 'I'm the film unit'—a slight exaggeration. The snotty wasn't impressed. 'Fuck the film unit' he said, and gave me an enormous push. I held my nose and jumped. I don't suppose the water wetted my ankles! Half a dozen staggers and I was ashore.

I joined up with Harry, and we found the main group already pinned down by pretty heavy enemy fire. Obviously our landing had not been the big surprise we had hoped. (It transpired afterwards that the German Commander had, by chance, had all his men turned out fully equipped that morning, no doubt to throw off the lethargy of Christmas, so our one day's delay ruined much of the preconceived tactics.)

The smoke was thinning, but the particles of burning sulphur had sunk deep into the snow, and gave off a weird Lower World light in the still early dawn. Harry set up the camera, and I, with my rifle, started scooting about, making short rushes, falling flat, pretending to fire, and so on. I had on battledress, with a woollen balaclava helmet, on top of which my tin hat perched somewhat precariously. As I had removed my War Correspondent flashes on the advice of an Intelligence Officer, who said the Germans immediately shot any found on such raids, I passed convincingly enough. Our shots caught the mysterious effect well and appeared in the official film. A sergeant soon spotted my charade, and grabbed the rifle off me for one of his men who had lost his on landing. (I did fire a real shot, however, much later on, when things were quiet. I borrowed a rifle, and shot some porcelain insulators off a telegraph pole, a thing I had always wanted to do since I had had an airgun.)

Although there was more machine-gun opposition at the

beach-head than expected, this was soon silenced by our Brens, and the main party set off for the centre of the town. The Germans had organized their defence in depth and extremely expertly. They scattered themselves into the houses in small groups, and fought the classic sniping and enfilading war of sudden bursts of fire from unexpected directions. They also defended their headquarters and the Ulveson Hotel next to it to the last man, which turned the initial battle into a much tougher and more destructive one than had been expected, with heavy casualties on both sides.

I was to see my first casualty soon, a magnificent looking young athlete, who was an Army boxing champion. Our beach was about half a mile from the centre of the little town, but between it and the town were a few scattered houses. The trouble was that no-one knew which held Germans, although all had civilians in them for sure. A new plan was formed, in which one group moved on the town across the high ground above it, while a second sneaked along the shore, protected by the overhanging boat-houses. A third small group was to reconnoitre the houses immediately in front of us. I watched them work their way forward to a farmhouse, flatten themselves against the walls, and then this young officer copied the technique seen in Westerns. Guns at the ready, he kicked the door in. But he forgot to jump back, and as the door swung open, he was smashed down with sub-machine-gun bullets. He had been in his first action about ten minutes. One of the negative statistics proven in this action was that the proportion of officers killed and wounded was far too high, and that you just cannot lead your men in the old-fashioned way without getting picked off.

We waited at the beach-head, where Command HQ and a casualty station had been set-up, until word came back that the advance parties had control of the centre of the town, so we set off to join them. I was shocked to meet Bill Lloyd, his face covered with blood, being helped to the casualty station. He seemed pretty dazed, and said he'd got it in the back. It turned out to be a false alarm, but I think it eventually led to his death. What had happened was that a German grenade had landed right behind him. The force of the explosion flung him forward, and a chunk of rock gave him a hell of a crack on his back. He smashed his face on the ground, and, with the pain behind, and his mouth and nose full of blood, he naturally imagined he had been hit in the lungs. When this was disproved he demanded to return to the battle, but the doctor refused to let him go. Bill almost cried with rage and frustration, and felt deeply he had let the Commandos down by reporting as wounded. Years later, while leading his section to capture a bridge in Sicily, he was severely wounded in both legs; but this time refused to be evacuated and insisted on being hoisted onto a bicycle and soldiering on. He died of loss of blood.

We found the main group bogged down in small groups around the centre of Vaagso. The principal strongpoints had been captured, but no-one quite knew where the Germans now were, although they were around all right, because you would be cosily sheltering behind some house, and suddenly a bullet would whistle past your ear, or worse, someone would be hit. The only thing to do was to mortar the houses, which, being wooden and heated by stoves, immediately burst into flames. So we didn't bring much Christmas cheer to the wretched citizens of Vaagso. The Germans were adept at skipping from one house to the other, but inevitably, some got shot in the process, and I was astonished to find they were wearing their gas masks. I never found out why—maybe the smoke—but British photographs of dead German soldiers with gas masks on would have been better propaganda for Germany than anything they could have cooked up themselves, so I had the grisly job of taking the masks off the corpses before we filmed them.

The next few hours remain for me as a series of cameo flashes, many tragic but some just plain funny, as any battle, big or small, seems to be. The first section we came across in the centre of the town was mortaring a villa from the shelter of a large brick wall. I left Harry to film this while I went to look for what was worthwhile photographing elsewhere. I found out they were going to blow up a tank they had dis-covered—used, by the look of it, strictly on Hitler's birthday only—and wandered back towards the mortar party. It was getting warmer, so I had undone my buttons and put my tin hat on the back of my head. I also had a fag on, and my hands in my pockets. As I rejoined Harry Rignold, he said, 'I got a marvellous shot of you walking back here—talk about Fred Karno's Army.' I paid no attention, merely saying 'Come on, they're going to blow up a toy tank.' Lap dissolve, as they say, to the private theatre of the War Office a week later, where the rushes were being run in front of every brass-bound desk wallah in Whitehall. I was hidden away in civvies, but I could hear their patter 'Jolly good smoke screen, eh? Congratulate your chaps, will you? Ah, some dead Jerries, that's what we like to see. Bloody efficient mortaring that', and suddenly I appeared, even scruffier than I had imagined, and, to a man, they all shouted 'Good God, *look* at that soldier!' I realized I did not even have a penknife to make me look military. I cowered in my seat, and had gone from the screen before they could say 'Take his name'. But, I can assure you, that shot did not appear in the official film.

We made our way to where I had found a couple of sappers, under a sergeant, crouching round a very small tank. Although the centre of the town was officially reported as having been cleared, there was still quite a bit of stuff whizzing around, so you progressed in a sort of Neanderthal crouch, interspersed with dashes worthy of hundred-yarders leaving their blocks.

As a piece of weaponry, the tank was pretty useless, but it was the first enemy object these engineers could legitimately destroy, so they were happily wiring up the explosives they had placed inside it. We prepared our camera, gave the nod, and there was a thump, some smoke, and a lot of bad language. The sergeant naturally came in for a good deal of ribbing from us and the odd bods who always seem to pop up at moments like this, battle or no battle. Stung in his professional pride, he promised he'd give us a marvellous film shot next time, if we'd hang on. But the buzz had gone out that the main body of engineers were going to blow up a sardine factory, so we moved on. Half an hour later we heard a shattering crash from the direction we had come, and we grinned at each other and said 'The old sarge made sure that time all right.' What we did not know until we got back on board that night was that he had made so sure and put so much jelly inside the tank, that it had burst like a grenade, and a big chunk of metal had cut him down, standing, apparently, just about where our camera had been.

As it was obvious that it was going to take some time to get all the charges laid in the fish factory, I left Harry to cover it, and made my way towards the lower part of the town, into which the Germans had been driven. On the way towards where heavy firing was still going on, I came across a couple of soldiers looking longingly into a fruit shop, whose only exhibit was a box of apples. We were all now famishing, but the debate was whether the apples were booby-trapped. We solved this by firing hundreds of rounds all around the box, and then gingerly extracting it from the window. Apart from slivers of glass, the apples tasted like blotting paper.

When I got to the street leading into the lower town, I found a section of Commandos holed up behind a temporary barrier, looking down into what was obviously the poorer part of the town. The houses were closer together, with only narrow alleyways between them, and sadly, many of them were well alight. Apparently, this section had tried to make their way down the street, but had been immediately fired on, and had retreated to the barrier. As usual, no-one quite knew where the enemy were hiding, so the mortars had been called in. The fire was jumping from one poor frame house to another and had soon spread across the street. Suddenly a German soldier broke from a burning house and made a dash for the other side. Every Commando fired of course, and halfway across, he staggered. His momentum kept him going, to fall right up against another burning building. There he lay and writhed. What happened then has often come back to me, sometimes in dreams. Everyone stopped firing, and we could see the young German—it was only about seventy yards away, so we could see he was young—frantically trying to crawl from the fire that was beginning to reach for him. But obviously his legs were paralysed, and he could not move himself. The flames began to lick around him, and he started to scream. The officer-in-charge of the Commandos asked for volunteers to go and rescue him, but no-one moved. I desperately wanted to volunteer, but funked it. I somehow felt that as I was there as a non-combatant, as someone who perhaps was more objective to war than professional soldiers,

I should have tried to save that wretched screaming creature. I still think I should have done it. I also think I would have been killed.

It was a long moment as the officer looked along the line of us, and then, slowly turning away as though accepting our verdict, he shot the young German dead.

I went back to where the sardine factory was at last ready for blowing, and when it did happen, we missed a marvellous shot that I imagine would have been another war classic. When the explosion went off, by some trick of the blast the whole roof lifted bodily, and out from under the eaves shot millions of the little oblong labels that cover the top of sardine cans. They flew high into the air like leaves in a sudden autumn flurry, and then floated gently down into the wreckage below. We were too close with our camera, and merely got the conventional collapse of the walls.

We had now met some of the people back from the attack on the fortified island, and learnt that, far from that being the really tough assignment, it had been almost a walk-over, and, at times, near farce. To start with, the garrison had thought the shelling was an air raid, so went into their shelters. A coastguard had suspected something was entering the fjord, but the German Commanding Officer's batman was cleaning his boss's boots, so didn't bother to answer the phone. At the moment we actually opened fire, a messenger was *rowing* across to warn them! It was gratifying to know that the Jerries could make bigger balls-ups than us. As a result of all this, the landing was virtually unopposed, and the Commandos only had two minor casualties. The other casualty was Jack Churchill, the piper, who had the bad luck to be leaning on a wall of the German barracks when one of his sappers blew it up from the other side!

Everything was now quiet around the centre of the town, and the battle had moved well into the lower part, when I heard a burst of fire about a hundred yards away, well over to my left, across an open green. I could see khaki figures crouching in a small grove of trees, and apparently firing at a large villa. I asked a senior officer what they were doing and he said casually, 'Arsing about, I should think—that area was cleared hours ago.' Thus encouraged, I set off across the park, hands in pockets as usual. As I got nearer, I could see that the target was a well-to-do two-storied house, with a large garden surrounded by a five-foot wire fence. The section of Commandos, who turned out to be reserves newly brought ashore, were concentrating their fire on the second-floor windows, from which all the glass and frames had been shot away. They were keeping very close cover behind some conveniently fallen trees.

In my new role of a veteran fighter—a film man becomes a self-made expert in anything he touches in ten minutes flat—I strolled up and, taking casual cover behind a tree, asked what was up. The very young lieutenant in charge, white with excitement, said 'There's two Jerries in that house.' I replied, patronizingly, 'The CO says this area was cleared hours ago.' The lieutenant spat at me, 'We saw them go in, damn you,' and started organizing an attack. I had seen so many false alarms and abortive attacks that morning that I still didn't believe him, so leant against my tree and thought 'Oh well, let him have his bit of fun'.

The lieutenant and his sergeant crawled to the fallen tree nearest the fence, and called for maximum covering fire. Everyone blazed away at the upper windows as the two leapt up and made a dash for the fence. They had just got one leg over it, when the sergeant jerked upright, hung for a moment, and fell back, dead.

I was down behind a tree almost as fast as that body, and, as one nearly always does, thought of myself first. 'Oh, Jesus, why didn't he shoot me? What a bloody stupid cocky idiot! Why, in God's name, didn't he let me have it?' The realization that I must have been in that sniper's sights all the way across the open, and while I stood there casually chatting, made me very frightened indeed. Looking back, maybe my unarmed scruffiness persuaded the sniper that I was a medical orderly or a stretcher bearer, but I didn't think of that at the time, and merely lay there and felt sick.

The job now was to get the lieutenant, who was desperately flattening himself behind about nine inches of raised rosebed, back to our side. I must say he kept his head admirably. He yelled to everyone to reload and then gave the order to fire. Then, with one bound—to use the classic phrase—he cleared the fence and fell amongst us untouched. The house was eventually burnt down and no-one came out. I imagine the Germans had skipped long before.

It was now time to withdraw. The Germans sniped at us, rather ineffectually, right back to the beaches. We left our dead but took with us 77 Norwegian volunteers, 98 German prisoners, some quislings, and two pathetic little trollops that had been found sleeping with the Germans. We had 20 killed and 57 wounded, mostly from No 3 Commando, so I again had to say goodbye to many friends. We also lost ten bombers and their crews.

In historical retrospect, it all seems a futile waste of fine young lives. Some shipping was sunk, some factories blown up, and some secret codes and ciphers captured. But most of the people of Vaagso were homeless, reprisals were taken all over Norway against the civilian population, and the Gestapo moved in with new repressions. Cynically, one can say that the Commandos, a kill-or-be-killed body, were properly blooded, that the propaganda value of the raid, in Britain and the world, was enormous, and that tens of thousands of German troops were kept watching the coasts instead of fighting on other fronts. Hating war as I now do, I still think it was a gallant useless gesture, with the only real memory those silent twisted bodies. Yet I must, of course, admit that I found those six hours on enemy territory infinitely stimulating and exciting, a time to boast about, to reminisce about, to laugh about, which is why, I suppose, men enjoy wars so much in retrospect.

The enemy made a half-hearted attempt to bomb us as we left, but the reaction had set in, and we, who had been ashore, just slept where we found ourselves. Being young, we soon recovered, and started swapping yarns and experiences. It was then I learned how tough the fighting had been around the enemy headquarters and the hotel, and how foolhardily brave the attacks were which finally captured them. Seeing the reporter from the agency wandering around, I asked him if I could see his piece. I had better explain that agency men, that is, people representing Reuters, United Press and so on, are not 'colour' writers. Their job is to send in factual reports, from which the various newspapers, by means of rewrite men and sub-editors, produce their feature stories. Being still full of the incredible experiences I had just heard, and the scenes I had witnessed, I found his stuff dry, stiff and unworthy. So when we got back to Aberdeen I sent a telegram to Christiansen at the *Express* saying 'Can give you exclusive authentic eye-witness report Vaagso raid, arriving tonight'. I swear I did not do this for gain or self-aggrandizement, but because I wanted to get the boys' efforts appreciated, and I knew I was fairly good at this sort of descriptive writing.

Chris grabbed me before I got drunk—we had been on strict rations for nearly two months—and I wrote my story, which I called 'They didn't bargain for "Knocker" White'. At three that morning Chris rang me to say that there were all sorts of rows at the Government censors about my article, and that he could not give me my by-line. I was in no state to care, and went back to sleep. What had rocked everything was my naïvely putting 'exclusive' in my telegram. It had gone to the Army Press Section, who were furious, other papers having to make do with the agency hand-out were furious, and I was carpeted. Chris had taken a chance and printed the article but by-lined it 'A composite picture of the Commando raid on Vaagso, gathered from several interviews by Morley Richards', one of his staff men. I imagine the 'composite' idea was put in to try and disguise from the other papers that the article had been specially written for him. The Army tried to frighten me, but I was back in civvies, and military men look a lot smaller from that position. Having read the story by this time, they knew it did them proud, so they calmed down, and let me off with a caution.

Although it obviously repeats a lot of what I have just written, I think it is worthwhile reprinting the article here to show how, for propaganda purposes, I made it all rather jolly and exciting like a Western, something I am now not proud of. But then it was our job, which we passionately believed in:

Daily Express 1st January 1942.
They didn't bargain for 'Knocker' White.
We had a heavy bashing going over. Those of us who weren't seasick tried to sleep, but the groaning of the ship

174

and the excitement kept us awake. We lay and smoked and made macabre jokes.

Towards six o'clock the sea got calmer, and we began to get ready. We'd all shaved and cleaned our boots the night before—uninstructed, with, I suppose, the idea of impressing the Norwegians with our smartness.

By seven land was in sight, a faint, sharp, dramatic silhouette, with already a lightening of the sky behind it. We steered straight towards it, and gradually our escort vessels began to take shape again.

By now we could see the entrance to the fjord. There was a sudden stir as a light appeared, but it turned out to be an automatic lighthouse. Action stations sounded and all guns were manned.

The sea was calm. The Commando troops waited quietly on the stairs below decks for the order to man the boats. There was no talking.

They were completely armed. Pockets and haversacks bulged with grenades. Tommy and Bren guns predominated. Each man had his fighting knife by his knee. Many officers had two revolvers.

By eight we had entered the fjord. We could see the high, rough cliffs, covered in most places by snow. In an odd bay snuggled a fisherman's hut. It was tricky navigating.

The leading ship turned and twisted under the direction of the Norwegian pilot. On the bridge our captain spoke quietly into the ship's telephone. Down below an adjutant received the message and nodded to the sergeant-major. He looked over his shoulder, jerked his head, and we followed. We were going into action. It was as simple as that.

Someone behind me whispered: 'Well, this is it, boys.' And then we were out on deck.

The assault landing-craft had been lowered to deck level. We handed over our weapons to the waiting sailors, stepped across the yard gap between the side of the ship and our boat, and then, taking back our guns, took our pre-arranged positions. In a minute we were afloat.

In the half light we formed up with landing-craft from the other transport. On the other side of the fjord, a cruiser majestically took up her position for the preliminary bombardment.

Up till now we saw no sign of the enemy. But just as our little armada turned towards the beaches, a Hampden came over low. And from the town pencils of tracer bullets went up.

At least they weren't asleep.

At the sight of the streams of bullets, the tearing crackle of the machine-guns, a tenseness could be felt in our boat. We knew we had to face that fire in less than a minute. and then from the boat alongside came the strains of the bagpipes, playing a fighting march.

In a flash the tension was gone. Someone whispered, 'The major's doing his stuff', and everyone grinned and we settled back quietly.

Then a cruiser opened up. Broadside after broadside echoed and rolled from cliff to cliff, from fjord to fjord. Maaloy island, a heavily armed little fortress, seemed to erupt. It was enveloped in flashes. By this time several Hampdens had arrived. The gunners fired at them furiously, but without effect.

From the edge of the town a series of Verey lights went up. By this time we could see our landing point. We had 100 yards to go.

Our armada split up. Half branched off towards the island, now a smoking ruin. Our bombardment stopped, and there was a momentary, uncanny silence. Then a machine-gun barked again, and we turned in to the beach.

The square front of the landing-craft went down and we stood up. This was our most vulnerable moment. Out of the narrow opening in our boat fully equipped men had to dash.

But this was combined operations. The Navy were landing us. The Air Force were there to help us, too. Out of the sky dived Hampden bombers, down past the cliffs to sea-level.

With a shattering roar they were over and past us. But in the split-second they were over us they released smoke bombs which burst on the rocks with showers of sparks.

Immediately we were enveloped in the fog. It was hell, but it was protection.

Because of it there was hardly a landing casualty. One man jumped too soon and had the unique experience of being run over by an invasion barge. Two were slightly wounded. But when the smoke got to the nearest German machine-gunner he packed up and retired.

Coughing, spluttering, cursing, and wet, we collected under the shore cliff. One landing craft caught fire and lit the whole scene with a ghostly flicker.

The striking parties set out. One group was to advance round the back of the town and cut off any retreat and then fight back towards the boats.

Another was to advance straight up the town to the German HQ, take that, and then make a house to house search while reserves would come up behind. Other groups were to search out isolated machine-gun nests.

As soon as our troops got to the edge of the smoke, they found that the opposition was going to be strong.

One small party dodged out of the smoke, and a bullet promptly nicked the funny-bone of the 20-year-old lieutenant in charge. He merely dodged back into the smoke, took another route and went on fighting all day.

Another group saw figures walking down a road. They waited until they were sure they were German, and then killed all five of them.

The troop that went up the back of the town, led by a 16 stone, 6ft 5in captain, early ran into concentrated machine-gun fire. They worked their way towards it, and eventually saw three Germans run into a hut.

The captain and his sergeant stormed it and shot two. The third dodged out of the back door and, unhappily, killed the captain as he turned to bring in his men. A Norwegian ran up and shot the German and did a war-dance of triumph when he had done so.

By this time the main party had reached the centre of the town after street fighting all the way.

The Germans sniped constantly and well all day. They were adepts at snap-shooting from windows and bushes.

And as their ammunition showed neither flash nor smoke they were very difficult to locate.

Many times in positions which appeared safe there would come a crack and a man would fall or the bullet would ricochet whining into the distance.

The Commandos were, of course, very handicapped by the fact that they wished to do as little damage to Norwegian property as possible.

A proper assault with artillery barrage would have taken the town in half an hour.

In the Ulverson Hotel, a large stone building, a strong force of Germans were surrounded. As they refused to surrender, the officer in charge of the attack went forward alone to throw grenades, but was killed by a machine-gun. He had consistently taken the main risks on himself.

This left his troop temporarily in charge of a cockney corporal, Knocker White, who proceeded to direct operations like a veteran, and succeeded in killing all the enemy in the hotel, despite three separate bullets through his haversack.

Meantime, things seemed to be well ahead on the island. As the smoke cleared we could see tiny khaki figures climbing the cliffs and hear bursts of Bren-gun fire. Then the ammunition dump blew up with a shattering roar and threw lumps of burning wood and rock clear over into the town.

On our side, too, the German ammunition hut caught fire. At first it seemed to be full of fireworks, and rockets and catherine wheels would come whizzing out past our heads and make us duck.

By this time stories of the battle began to circulate. I met an Australian officer coming weaving up the main street. He had been sniped in the back from a house they had to pass to get to their objective.

He told me that the Germans were fighting for every inch of the town, and were deadly shots. It turned out afterwards they were a regiment specially trained in sniper fighting.

One of them hid in a rowing boat and drifted down behind us. A sergeant sank the boat with a Bren-gun. Others had taken to the woods behind the town and continued to snipe from there all day. In fact, the boats and HQ were under desultory fire all the time.

The party that set out round the back of the town had considerable opposition all the way, but pressed on resolutely under their one remaining officer, the brother of the leader who had been killed, and gained their objective.

They spotted a sniper high in the cliffs above them and got him first shot with an anti-tank rifle. He stood up and then fell headlong 200ft to the ground. Another sniper fell from a window as he was hit.

By now the centre of the town round the Ulverson Hotel was ablaze, and the main body of the enemy had fallen back. But advance was still difficult. Practically every house was a strong-point. A reserve troop was brought up and went into action. The first objective of a section of them was a wooden house where it was suspected three Germans were hiding.

From behind the scanty cover of a tree we lay and fired a small mortar. The gunner was aiming at a window, and the rest of his section made ribald comments at his shooting whenever he missed.

After a few hits the Scots lieutenant in charge decided to attack.

The house was surrounded by a strong six-foot high wire fence. The section took it like kangaroos. But just as it all appeared to be over there was a double crack from the house. A sergeant dropped from the top of the fence and lay still. By this time the lieutenant was halfway across the garden. He crouched behind the raised earth of a flower bed and signalled to the rest to give him covering fire. Then he raised himself on his elbow and lobbed a couple of grenades. They shattered the walls of the house. Two more and the house caught fire. No Germans came out.

Back in the town the demolition squads had arrived, casually pushing a go-cart filled with explosives. A wheel came off in a rut and 600lb of death and destruction poured across the road. The sappers cursed cheerfully and carried it on past the fires on their backs.

A few prisoners and quislings were coming in, some

helping to carry British wounded. As the firing went up the town some friendly Norwegians appeared from their cellars. One Norwegian woman carrying a baby was sniped as she crossed the road. She fell forward and the child slipped from her arms into the snow, where it lay crying. Other Norwegians dragged it into a doorway.

All this time we had had uninterrupted air support. But now the syncopated banging of a 'Chicago Piano' from a destroyer made us look up. And what we saw made us duck. Two Me 109s were diving down on us from the sun and machine-gunning the streets.

No-one was hit and the Me's never appeared again.

From time to time bombers came over high and tried to bomb the ships, but failed completely. They were usually chased away by the Beaufighters that took the place of the Hampdens and Blenheims. Altogether the RAF played an essential and extremely efficient part in the whole operation.

The progress of the operation was now clear. The island was completely subdued. The prisoners from it were evacuated and a series of explosions marked the beginning of the demolitions.

Gun emplacement after gun emplacement went up in bits and splattered the sea around like a shoal of mackerel breaking the surface.

Our little colonel decided to go through the town and take charge.

He and his headquarters entourage marched up the street as though going on an inspection. He seemed to bear a charmed life. A German put a stick grenade at his feet, and although two men were wounded he was untouched.

Our demolitions started, explosive lifted the roof of a fish canning factory, and out from under it blew an enormous shower of tin labels that went high in the air and then fluttered down among us like a pamphlet raid.

The Germans' only tank, used, it turned out, mostly for propaganda effect, was blown up and spread across the hillside. The radio station disappeared. Another factory went on fire.

Vaagso as a war asset was finished. And so were the

Germans. Apart from a few snipers hidden in the high-treed hills behind the town, they were either killed or prisoners.

The order to retire was given. Back came the troops, many carrying German tin hats or weapons as trophies. Some, lightly wounded, limped on the arms of their pals. Others chewed apples they found in a demolished fruit shop.

It was the only Christmas fare they'd had. All were cheery and reckoned they'd had a 'good show'.

As they assembled at the rendezvous the beach officer, a naval man dressed in a battle-dress top and bell-bottomed trousers, ordered them to their craft by megaphone. Some of the troops mimicked him as they scrambled down the rocks. 'This way for the *Skylark*. Twice round the fjord a tanner.' But they boarded quickly and in perfect order.

And all the time a persistent sniper from the hills would every now and then make a bullet ping among us. Luckily he was their one bad shot.

Finally the fighter screen protecting our withdrawal was called in and the little fleet sailed off for our depot ships.

We were entertained on the way back by a dignified duel between a cruiser and a mobile Germany battery that had opened fire from the mainland. It was all very precise. They fired and missed, we fired and missed; they fired and almost hit, we fired and hit.

We had a few side bets on the way back to pass the time. Once alongside, the reaction began to set in. We noticed how cold we were and how tired. But we could not go below. We hung around the decks and grinned at the rather bewildered Norwegians we were taking back.

The convoy formed up and we began snaking out of the fjord again. The sun was going down and had left the valleys, but high on the hills it whitened the snow and contrasted it sharply with the pall of heavy smoke left by our fires.

At the mouth of the fjord we were surprised to find a ship on fire. This turned out to be a German coaster that had got the surprise of its life, when it had sailed into the bay all unsuspecting and practically collided with a British destroyer. It promptly ran aground.

As we left each ship had a crack at it for luck. It was left resembling a colander.

On the way back we had a couple of half-hearted bombing attacks, but they all fell clear. By that time we were all so tired and blasé that we didn't even bother to go on deck. The only comment I heard was an officer who dropped a sandwich when the bombs fell and who ejaculated indignantly, 'What the hell do they think they're trying to do? Spoil my supper?'

But most of us just went to sleep. We'd had a busy day.

There is a very little footnote to this storm in a teacup about my 'exclusive'. Many years later I was browsing through books heaped on a barrow in some market. I picked up one called, I think, *Great Stories of the War*, and there was my 'Knocker White' bit, only it was credited solely to Mr Morley Richards. The best of British luck to him.

I wrote a Commando script, but it was much too ambitious for the Ministry of Information to tackle, so I was loaned out to Gaumont-British to see if they would like to make it. I was allocated a 'professional' script-writer, to show the poor little amateur the mysterious ways of the mighty. As he immediately wanted to inject into my story a pretty ATS girl, a glamorous Norwegian spy, and a clutch of brave little wives holding the fort at home, I lasted about three weeks.

7

I was equally unhappy when I got back to the Crown Film Unit. We had lived for so long as a tight, rather mad, family, constantly quarrelling together, yet always completely loyal, and sparking off from each other a constant stream of ideas and creative impulses. I know now that I was one of the most difficult ones. I had been accustomed to bursting in on Cavalcanti with half a dozen ideas, all of which I was convinced were as great as the invention of the wheel. Cav would gently disillusion me, and when I got childishly recalcitrant, would say something like 'OK, Harry, quit if you want to—but young Pat is having trouble with that last sequence, why don't you just have a look at it first?', and I would trot off happily to the cutting-rooms, and everyone would forget my boring tantrums.

I found our new producer, Ian Dalrymple, cold, distant, and generally discouraging—to me at any rate. So I stopped putting up ideas, and, I suppose, sulked. There was something else worrying me as well. That was, where should we go from where we were? Jack Holmes, Humphrey Jennings and I had got to about the limit of what we could do with amateur actors. While they were utterly convincing portraying their own jobs, or even their way of life, they obviously lacked the skill to rise beyond that. Bernard Miles, in an article in *Documentary News Letter* written about that time, analysed this problem so well, that I would like to quote him at some length:

'In all the documentary films that I have seen', he writes, 'and I have seen some dozens in the past three or four weeks apart from isolated examples in the course of ten years' steady cinema going, I think that non-actors achieve all, or at any rate most, that the very best professional actors could achieve in the same circumstances. But this is only because most of these pictures avoid the implications of human action, or where they do present it, present it in such a fragmentary way as never to put to the test the training and natural qualities which differentiate an actor from a non-actor. It seems to me that in this lies the whole crux of the matter, because when I say that documentary has never faced up to the problem of sustained characterization and development on the human side of its material, I am simply implying that the leaders of documentary are guilty of a kind of escapism, a deliberate side-stepping of the very central problem in that interpretation of reality which is their avowed aim, I mean Man and his efforts to find his bearings in the universal set-up.

'. . . in documentary film, man is nearly always implicit but rarely explicit. It seems that documentary insists upon placing the major emphasis upon circumstances and environment and only by inference upon the human being as an individual. I contend that this is a limitation and a cul-de-sac which documentary directors will sooner or later find themselves forced to revolt against. Man's hopes, his doubts, his fears, his yearnings, his aspirations . . .—from all these documentary seems to turn away—only the economic and natural forces which condition his behaviour and set the scene of the struggle, but never the struggle itself. Always the circumference, never the centre.

'It seems to me that documentary displays with the greatest clarity the material world and the environment in which all our problems have to be solved, that it shows with equal clarity most of the problems themselves, but that it makes little or no attempt to grapple with the most important thing of all, the act of solution. To this extent documentary is a passive rather than an active medium. But I suggest that true social analysis can have only one object—action towards the solution of the problems analysed. And I further suggest that these inescapable social and propagandist aims can best be served, from the screen point of view, by a marriage of documentary as we know it, with a more and ever more human story value and by an ever-increasing concentration upon people. And that this can best be achieved by the isolation of the particular typical people, and that for this purpose actors trained to portray the development of human character and the intensification of thought and feeling that go with it, will have to be used more and more.'

Those were the dilemmas that were buzzing in my head, although in no such lucid or logical form, and I had no conceivable thought of leaving the Crown Unit. I was therefore utterly taken aback, when after a row with Dalrymple and a threat to resign, he calmly said 'All right, Harry, we'll call it the end of the month, shall we?' I was shocked—my bluff had been called, and it was like a blow in the solar plexus. Yet I hadn't the guts to back down.

There were now plenty of opportunities to join feature films, but my flirtations with them had not been encouraging, to put it mildly, and the crazy over-inflated episodes connected with *Target for Tonight* and *Eagle Squadron* had shown me how phoney and ephemeral that side of the film business was. So I did not go dancing off with my head in the clouds, looking to see my name in lights—though, as it happened, I finally did. I followed Cavalcanti to Ealing Studios, where they were beginning, partly due to his influence, to make the fine realist films—documentary was always a pedantic word—that were to give it such a distinguished record.

Well, there it was. I had suddenly left behind me the best twelve years of my life.

When I came to bid goodbye, Stewart McAllister, the Scots editor, who had never been known to pay a compliment, said something that I've always treasured. He said 'You know, Harry, you've got something—I'm buggered if I know what it is—but you've got something'.

I would be happy to have that as an epitaph.

*   *   *   *   *

Did I achieve anything? As I have said, I had imagined that I had only contributed one or two cinematic moments worth remembering. But recently, all my old films of thirty years were run to refresh my memories and, by God, do you know, I think I had an influence on British cinema. Not me alone, of course, but Jack Holmes, Pat Jackson, Humphrey Jennings and Jack Lee, all of us who developed the story documentary. Through some unsuspected theatrical trait, no doubt inherited from my father's loud checks and extraordinary cravats, I drew documentary away from the accepted assemblage of visuals tied together with a commentary, to a dramatized, more human approach. However, when it comes to our definite influence on the feature film industry, don't let's kid ourselves about our creative impact. War was our bonus, as was the sudden shock that our kind of film was actually taking more money at the box-office than theirs. Although documentary remained a dirty word, realism became accepted as the basis for many films. As Parker Tyler, an American film critic of the time, has said, 'Journalism crept into the techniques of American and British films'. Such war pictures as *The Foreman Went to France, San Demetrio London, The Way Ahead* and *The Cruel Sea* were direct descendants of *North Sea, Target for Tonight, Merchant Seamen* and *Fires Were Started*. And it went on, although how much our work was influential is hard to say. There were the tremendous Italian post-war films, like *Open City*. There was the excitement when American features went out into the cities and the streets with films like *Naked City* and *Boomerang*. Most of such techniques and realist ideas have now been taken over by television, at times superbly well. It would seem that the film trade has returned to one of its original premises, that the impulse to think is not necessarily the impulse to buy.

John Grierson once said, 'Documentary is a clumsy description, but let it stand.' I think it has stood.

* * * * *

The move over to Ealing was quite painless. It was a small, compact, self-contained unit run on paternalistic, communal lines by Michael Balcon. Under him there were half a dozen directors and associate producers, who formed interchangeable teams to make specific pictures, and who, once they got the go-ahead, worked pretty much on their own. These directors and associate producers were mostly about my age and, surprisingly, equally scruffy-looking. They greeted me casually, accepted me into their little heirarchy, and the only difference I could find at first to my previous film life was that I now regularly drank whisky, and had much less to do. Although it all seemed very egalitarian, there were some odd class differences. There were three dining-rooms, for instance. The snob one for Balcon, his eminence grise the money man, Major Baker, the studio manager and visiting VIPs. Then there was a dining-room for us, plus certain heads of departments, such as casting, scenario and the art department, but not the chief electrician or the head property man. They ate with the workers in the main canteen. Certain of us, from time to time, started to eat in the canteen, but the food was so awful, we soon forgot our principles and returned to our fold. The class consciousness that trade unionism brings about also soon struck me. Although we were all, from top to bottom, on a first-name basis, the upper echelons could not presume on this. When, on *Nine Men*, my first film for Ealing, I called an electrician the kind of thing we in documentary had been calling each other daily, I nearly had a strike on my hands. Yet, within one's own stratum, you could call anyone anything you wanted.

Another new phenomenon for me was the publicity department. Although we had had in Grierson one of the great publicists in the world, we rank and filers never sought publicity or received it until it was thrust upon us by the success of our war films. At even a small commercial studio like Ealing, there was fierce competition for credits, and through them, publicity, because that led to recognition, prestige, better jobs—and more money. In documentary we had been pretty casual about credits, never mentioning, for instance, that in ninety per cent of cases the director had also written the script. This came about, I imagine, as part of Grierson's original do-it-yourself type of teaching and was a great mistake. He had just said 'Make a film about so-and-so', and expected you to do everything. This was at a time when we were associating with the best of a crop of fine progressive writers, who could have rubbed away our naïveté, and perhaps given our films the social bite they lacked, a point which present-day realist film-makers are quick to point out.

187

The Ealing publicity department was run by a gloriously funny character with the unbelievable name of Moyna Danischewsky. He hated his job, but was about the best one at it in the business. He hated it because he constantly saw how publicity affected simple people. He once said a thing which I have quoted ever since: 'Publicity is worse for the soul than sex or drink.' He watched the sweet little starlets arrive straight from repertory or drama school, started telling the world how intelligent they were, how glamorous they were, how domesticated they were, what they wore, what they ate, what books they read, who was mad about them, and so on, and he knew the stupid little cows would believe their own utterly phoney publicity, and so turn into egocentric, conceited, mannered bitches.

It was Danny, as he was always known, who persuaded me to go to Ealing, as he had done with Cavalcanti. He also found Tibby Clarke, the writer of the great Ealing comedies, in obscurity in Fleet Street, and Sandy McKendrick, later to be a world-class director, struggling with cheap publicity films in Wardour Street. This was Michael Balcon's greatest asset—he listened to the advice of the people he employed, and took a chance with relatively unknown creative people. Because they were eager, sincere, and anxious to succeed, they hardly ever let him down, and built up Ealing Studios into a world name in international cinema out of all proportion to its size and budget.

Once I had been accepted into the little community, and allocated an office—the place was so small we always had to share offices—I was more or less forgotten, and left to my own devices. This is a common phenomenon with studios of whatever size. They love to buy people, and then often don't quite know what to do with them. Pat Jackson was an example of this. When his classic *Western Approaches* film came out in 1945 he was signed up by Korda to go to Hollywood for MGM. By the time he got to America, Korda and MGM had split and he spent five mainly frustrated years in Hollywood, making one 'B' class picture. However, MGM was once taken for a beautiful ride by Hecht and McArthur, the famous writing team. As a parting gift, they sold their tennis instructor to the studio as an eminent English man of letters. Duly ensconced in an office at 1,000 dollars a week, the bloody fool could well have been there yet, if he hadn't insisted on trying to write!

During my idle days at Ealing, I had, perhaps for the first time, a chance to look back at my film career, and speculate on where it was going. When contemplating or analysing the British documentary movement of the thirties and forties, you at once return to the strange, ambivalent character of John Grierson. He had one of the strongest, most compelling personalities that I have ever met, and yet I don't think he was a strong man. He had the quality of an evangelist, which made it difficult to question his theories and beliefs. (Even while writing this book, so many years on, I feel a vague discomfort when I criticize him, like a schoolboy writing about his headmaster.) It was his evangelism that made him want power—not riches or position, but converts. I believe it was this search for power that took him away from the GPO, which, with the hindsight of the war, was a great mistake. It has been put about by his disciples that he left in order to have the freedom to make films of more social significance. But, historically, this is just not true. The two best films of social criticism of that period *Housing Problems* and *Enough to Eat* had been made prior to Grierson's departure from the GPO. And, in my opinion, few films came out of any of the bodies he set up all over the world—always with one of his key men in charge—to match the consistent standard of the GPO and Crown Film Unit productions.

The trouble with his leadership for simple film-makers like me was that he theorized too much. It's a well-known weakness of prophets, that when you dare to analyse their writings and sayings, you often find an awful lot of doubletalk. Art is instinctive, and it also needs an instinctive ability to create it. This has nothing to do with intelligence. Grierson was tremendously intelligent, vibrant, virile, a world authority on cinema. But, to me, he was not basically a film-maker, but an instigator.

The decision of Cavalcanti, myself, Jennings and the others to stay on at the GPO Unit, and concentrate on the dramatized realist film was actually following one of Grierson's beliefs that 'Documentary would not have succeeded if it did not influence

189

cinema as a whole'. To us that meant what it meant to the man in the street—the commercial cinema. It was incredible cheek of us to take on such a task, and, as I have said, would not have succeeded if war had not come. But we didn't funk it.

It was logical, therefore, that some of us should join the commercial boys when, at last, after years of patronizing superiority, they actually wanted us to teach them something. Looking back now, although my career with them was considered a success, I regret it. The big time saps your values, no matter how hard you battle. On the other hand, documentary died after the war. The prehensile grip of the ever increasing civil servants had overwhelmed the Crown Film Unit, and reduced it to an overstaffed, over-administered frustration. (Around 1948, I was approached by the last of the old stagers left at Crown to go back and take over. Although the salary was derisory, I at once agreed, and went to see the appropriate Ministry officials. I asked for two conditions; the right of hiring and firing, and the right to divide up the total film budget amongst the films as I thought most worthwhile, rather than accepting their allocations. They refused point blank.)

The Crown Film Unit was eventually closed down by the government, a dreadful, thoughtless act, even if it had become top-heavy and unproductive. Dramatized documentary got one last chance through private enterprise, when in 1951 the National Film Finance Corporation set up Group Three. This provided ample funds for the making of second-feature films with a guaranteed release, the emphasis being on the employment of young, rising directors, technicians and writers. What an opportunity this was for us to prove our theories by practical demonstration once and for all! I hopefully applied for the job, but Grierson got it, in partnership with a very old-time director, John Baxter, who had been living for twenty years on his enormous success with Walter Greenwood's *Love on the Dole*.

It is obviously leading with my chin to say now that Group Three was a disaster, but the trade, that first arbiter of things cinematic, will confirm it. The films were mostly old-fashioned, snobbish and second-rate. And don't forget some of the greatest films the world has seen started as cheap second-features, like *The Ox-Bow Incident*, *The Informer* and *Marty*. Eventually, the scheme petered out, after losing hundreds of thousands of pounds, and what I consider was one of the most far-sighted gestures ever made for British cinema was dissipated by conforming to, of all things, the vulgar taste of Wardour Street.

What of documentary today? It is, of course, practically wholly made for television. But the word has been so bastardized and cheapened, that it now covers anything from re-photographed postcards to nature study travelogues. What I find most surprising is the almost total lack of improvement in film-making techniques since our day, despite the incredible advance in modern equipment and the ease of working. Daily we get flung at us great chunks of film footage loosely tied together with commentary obviously spoken to the cutting copy, and then happily married in the laboratory. We treated commentary like music, and recut the picture to the words, so that there was always counterpoint and rhythm between the two. And those talking heads. How I hate that constant succession of talking heads! If only the film-makers would call themselves reporters or journalists, good honest names but no, they must all be documentarists. I realize of course that the constant rush to supply television with material makes impossible any chance of putting polish to most of their productions.

In cinema, our type of documentary is almost dead—but not quite. In the 1950s there was the fascinating series of experimental films, called Free Cinema, inspired by people like Lindsay Anderson and Carol Reisz, both of whom have gone on to international reputations. They took advantage of the new facilities for shooting, and with hand-held and hidden cameras got natural behaviour of people *en masse* that has never been bettered. What was most remarkable—and admirable—was the amount of social criticism they got into their films. This has been the sorest point between us originals and present-day realist film-makers. They basically despise us for the political timidity in our work. And they have a point. Here we were, in the midst of the greatest Depression of all time, mostly showing workers bravely carrying on with their wonderful skills, and hardly ever mentioning that they were underpaid, underfed and appallingly housed. Our answer is, of course, that just by showing, for the first time, the achievement, the essential and overwhelming contribution of the ordinary man to society, we would give them a pride and a realization of their strength that would encourage them to act on their own behalf. This is a weak and specious argument. The truth is that if we had indulged in real social criticism to any extent, we would have immediately been without sponsorship and our whole experiment, which was artistically a fine one, would have finished. So we compromised.

One development in documentary in the sixties has been Cinema Verité. Its protagonists believe that the only real truth that can be caught by the camera is spontaneous, unrehearsed behaviour. They say that if you synthesize any story or event, or recreate it with actors or even with the real people, then it is merely your personal interpretation, and therefore false. Everything must be photographed or recorded as it happens. Propagandized a great deal in America and France—although it is based on the theories of the Russian director Vertov in the 1920s—it is now the favourite theory amongst the students of the new film schools which have been created just as the film industry is dying. They've often had a go at me, so I think I'm entitled to have a go at them. I think their theory is as phoney as a four-dollar bill. I admit, of course, that in moments of violence or panic, nothing can compare with recorded reality. But they put out whole films, claiming them to be spontaneous. One unit went into a factory during an industrial dispute, and filmed for a month. Their first viewing copy—for an hour-long film—lasted thirty-two hours! So then they started cutting, selecting, and rejecting, in fact making their own personal interpretation of the material.

A famous Cinema Verité picture of an ordinary family's life together got extremely good notices on television, but when I questioned the director, he admitted he had advertised for families, and had eventually chosen the one for its filmic possibilities. So at once it was not Cinema Verité. I consider it lazy, unprofessional film-making, brought about by the ease of shooting that fast stock, hand-held cameras, radio mikes and so on have provided.

There are still glimpses of hope. Quite recently, Ken Loach opened the way again for using amateur actors in films of the feature length and shocked that most constipated of bodies, Cinema Exhibitors, when *Kes* became an unexpected box-office smash. And in 1972, a Scots boy, Bill Douglas, having been given a few quid to experiment with by the British Film Institute, came up with a staggeringly realistic and moving film *My Childhood*. Using the actual people of his mining village, he combined our old technique of dramatic reconstruction with the modern freedom of shooting to give an unforgettable picture of poverty in our time. He's a boy we must watch and help, because a first success is a heavy burden to bear.

I had been at Ealing over a month, and was beginning to get worried, when Angus McPhail drifted into my office, threw a couple of pages of typescript onto my desk and said casually 'This might be your cup of tea—let me know' and drifted out again. Angus McPhail was another of the delightful eccentrics that populated Ealing Studios at that time. Very tall and cadaverous, he was perfect casting for the absent-minded professor, with an enormous nose that balanced the prominent Adam's apple on his long thin neck. He was immensely erudite, with high academic honours, but had somehow got caught up in films. Punctually at nine o'clock every morning he arrived to work extremely quickly and efficiently on such epics as the Will Hay and Gracie Field comedies. Just as promptly, at six o'clock in the evening, he marched straight over to the Red Lion across the road, and drank doubles until eight. He then started to curse us as sycophants, whores and hypocrites. Knowing he was cursing himself and loving him very dearly, we used to lead him to the waiting hire-car that took him home. It was the days of the famous Kruschen Salts advertisements, in which you were exhorted to take daily enough salts to cover a sixpence in order to stay fighting fit. Once, when an intrepid journalist asked Angus how he managed to stay so fresh on his somewhat extreme régime, he replied in his quiet cultured voice 'My dear boy, I always take enough Kruschen Salts to cover a pound note'.

What Angus had given me was a two-page outline for a short Army training film, written by Gerald Kersh, a writer who had had a considerable success with a book about the Guards, called *They Died With Their Boots Clean*. Although I didn't like the writing, I thought there was the germ of a very good idea in it and I asked permission to try and work it up to feature length. Everybody was obviously delighted to find something for me to do, so I settled down to what was to be the screenplay of *Nine Men*. Ealing, being an adventurous and intelligent studio, were anxious to experiment in dramatized reality, but were still strangely unaware of our basic idea. However, they let me go my way, and *Nine Men* with a cast of amateurs, semi-amateurs, professionals and semi-professionals, and an astonishingly low cost of £20,000, went out as a first feature, and made Ealing a fortune. It started me on a career of another eleven years there, which took me round and round the world at somebody else's expense, the original dream of that B.Com. (failed) at Edinburgh University so long ago. My films became known at Ealing as 'Watt's Tropical Tours' and, as I've astonished myself in getting this book written, I might even write about them some day.

This account of my early years is in no way a history of the documentary film movement. Indeed, I am pretty certain that if those pundits who always seem to rise up around the periphery of any art movement, and, by writing and commenting on it, often make a far better living than the artists ever did, should read this, they will tear their hair. This has only been, for better or worse, the personal experiences of a brash, overbearing, cheeky and opinionated youngster who unexpectedly got the chance to make films.

Index